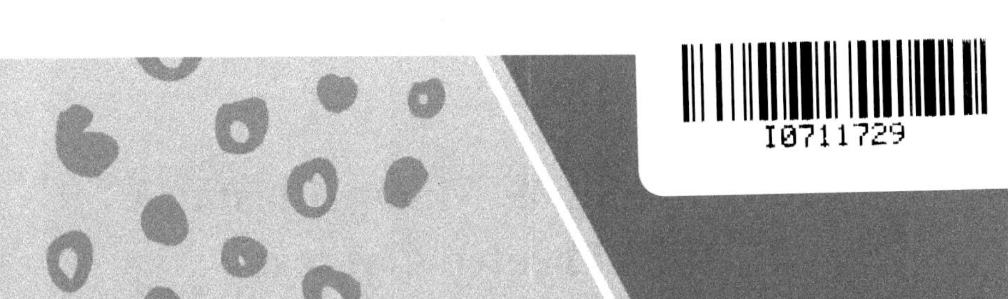

CODESWITCHING & MALAPROPISM: A MULTI-FACETED CONTEXT

A COMPENDIUM OF REVIEW PAPERS

Michael L. Estremera, Ph.D.

Codeswitching & Malapropism: A Multi-Faceted Context

A Compendium of Review Papers

Michael L. Estremera

Published by Lulu Press Inc.
United States of America
ISBN 978-1-6780-2604-2

DEDICATION

This book is dedicated to my parents Lucia L. Estremera and Benjamin E. Estremera (deceased) for instilling good values and the fighting spirit to never falter despite the hardships along the way --- the seemingly insurmountable and unreachable goals in life, for after the rain comes the rainbow.

To my siblings Merly Estremera-Gonzales, Ma. Marisa Estremera-Laguna, Federico L. Estremera, Mirasol Estremera-Rescobillo, Manuel L. Estremera, Maribel Estremera-Barnido, and Myrna L. Estremera for their support that fueled the author to step-up against the odds

I also dedicate this great achievement to my friends (Mike, Bry, Ren, Kaye, Cherry, Omar, Boyet, Bert, Del,…) in good times and in bad times.

I likewise devote this piece of work to my Sorsogon West family for the culture of excellence being cultivated in this performing district, special mention to my caliber Public Schools District Supervisors, Ma. Teresa B. Hapita and Mr. Antonio Jintalan.

To my Alma Mater which contributed much to this masterpiece; Marinas Elementary School, St. Anthony Academy, Abuyog National High School, Sorsogon State College, and Annunciation College of Bacon Sorsogon Unit Inc., for nurturing and honing my skills holistically.

To my co-teachers in Tugos Elementary School, Sorsogon West District; Charity Gerolia-Loar, Sharon Rosin-Donor, Consolacion Laid-Bio, Leilani Barba-Fabia, Judy Lopez-Liwanag, Josie Espineda-Casiao, and Mary-Grace Ladimo-Pura for their commendable work ethics and praiseworthy initiatives relevant to the DepEd's programs.

My former co-teachers and pupils in Marinas I Elementary School, the same school which developed my hidden skills in journalism as well as in arithmetic, this book is wholeheartedly devoted to all of you.

ACKNOWLEDGEMENTS

The author wishes to express his gratitude to his master's degree students in the summer class of 2021 for their significant help in realizing this abstract goal of writing a book.

MARCLETTE E. VILLAPANDO
Sorsogon National High School
marclette.villapando@deped.govph

BEN P. LACAY
Abuyog National High School
ben.lacay@deped.gov.ph

MARIA THERESA D. ATUTUBO
Sorsogon National High School
mtcda1989@gmail.com

MAY ANN D. DIO
Sorsogon National High School
mayann.dio@deped.gov.ph

ELIZABETH D. ENDONELA
Annunciation College of Bacon
Sorsogon Unit, Inc.
elizabethendonela59@gmail.com

PHILIP FLORES
Sorsogon National High School
philip.flores@deped.gov.ph

MYLAH S. HERNAN
Sorsogon National High School
mylah.hernan@deped.gov.ph

RONNALYN N. JALMASCO
Bogña Integrated School
ronnalyn.jalmasco@deoed.gov.ph

TITAN JOY S. SAN DIEGO
Gallanosa National High School
titanjoyssandiego@gmail.com

RANJEE F. TEJADA
Gabao National High School
Ranjee.tejada@deped.gov.ph

CHRISTIAN REY S. GRAGAS
Irosin North High School
chrisstianrey.gragas@deped.gov.ph

DEOVELITA D. FORTES
Gabao National High School
Gabao, Irosin,Sorsogon
deovelita.fortes@deped.gov.ph

KRISTINE G. TERRADO
Gabao National High School
kristine.terrado@deped.gov.ph

TABLE OF CONTENTS

FOREWORD

Colonization and English Language

Phillipson (1992) scrutinized the probable reasons linked to English as the world's most dominant language. He claimed that the spread of English was not unpremeditated but, in effect, carefully planned. In one of his books, he highlighted how the cultural and commercial undertakings of the colonizers played a pivotal function in determining the cultural symbol (e.g., Indian culture). Conversely, Pennycook (1998) argues that the colonial discourse around English and English culture may have been exploited to substantiate colonial and imperial economic activities.

Still, these conversations about the superiority of the former and the latter's inferiority are not common reactions of the material domain. These could have been manifestations of cultural discourse itself. To supplement, Calvet (1987) recognized two contributory steps to linguistic colonization. In Vertical step is connected to the social spread of the English language. The European language first spread into the upper classes of the colonized people. Horizontal step, conversely, has to do with the geographical spread of language. The colonial language is diffused from the capital to the small cities and, from there, to the villages.

The colonizers mainly spend much effort through the educational system to instill this asymmetrical social ideology in their social and linguistic practices. This has likewise been underpinned by Spencer (1985), who conjectured that the colonizer's language became necessary for all those who wished to advance socially and participate in the colony's public sphere. This is true to the socially upward people who quickly eschewed the local languages and to favored the colonial language. The educated increasingly opted to raise their children in a colonial language rather than an African language.

Moreover, colonization and the slave trade also led to the creation of new languages. The most well-known and studied cases are the Creole languages in European plantation societies worldwide [Carrebean, America, and Australia]. Coming from diverse social and linguistic backgrounds, their creators- such as African slaves and European indented laborers in the case of Pacific creoles (Mint & Price, 1976 and 1992).

Similarly, Holm (1989), Mufwene (2015), and Muhleisen (2010) hypothesized that due to their having emerged as a direct consequence of European slavery, their surface resemblance to the colonial language, and their encounter with populations of low reputation, Creole was held in contempt by the Europeans. They are mostly not recognized as languages in their own right but are considered make-shift languages and flawed or corrupted versions of the colonial language.

Metaphysics of Malapropism and Code-switching

There is much argument in linguistics concerning the dissimilarity between code-switching and language transfer (Treffers, 2009). In effect, the concerns of the use of code-switching as a medium of instruction in the context of English as Foreign Language (EFL) classes may have been deliberated already for many years since code-switching is deemed the last recourse used in multilingual Asians such as Indonesia (Liu, 2010; Mujiono, Poedjosoedarmo, Subroto, & Wiratno, 2013).

In some circumstances, linguists denote the benefits and disadvantages of language transfer as two separate phenomena, i.e., language transference and language interference, correspondingly (Brice, 2015). In such interpretations, these two kinds of language transfer and code-switching can encompass what is known as a cross-linguistic influence (Brice, 2015). To some degree, an instance of discourse error is called a malapropism when a word is produced that is irrational or ridiculous in context, yet similar in sound to what was intended (Fay, 1982). Malapropisms vary from other kinds of speaking or writing errors, such as eggcorns or spoonerisms, and from the unintentional or cautious production of newly made-up words (neologisms) Zwickky, 1982). For instance, it is not a malapropism to use obtuse [wide or dull] instead of acute [narrow or sharp]; it is undoubtedly deemed a malapropism to use obtuse [stupid or slow-witted] when one means abstruse [esoteric or difficult to understand]. Malapropisms usually maintain the part of speech of the initially intended word.

Similarly, substitutions tend to have the same number of syllables and metrical structure – the same form of stressed and unstressed syllables – as the envisioned word or phrase. If the stress pattern of the malapropism varies from the intended word, unstressed syllables could be deleted or inserted; stressed syllables and the collective rhythmic patterns are maintained (Sheridan, 2005). Moreover, malapropisms, of course, are so named from Mrs. Malaprop (from the French mal à propos, or inappropriately), a character from Richard Sheridan's The Rivals, who was wont to use wrong words that occurred to sound like the ones she wanted to utter ("He is the very pine-apple of politeness!" -> pinnacle).

Though it's regularly regarded as stemming from ignorance, especially when politicians are making these amusing blunders, it's honestly a common communication error that can transpire even if the speaker knows the lexical definitions of the e words entirely. In the same vein, we may unsurprisingly make other semantic speech mistakes, such as anticipating what we mean to say in our heads and puzzlingly replacing it with its opposite. We may also substitute the word with a related word ("Don't burn your fingers"/"Don't burn your toes") or in an even more perplexing use of another word that sounds like a related word (heritage/legacy -> heresy) (https://bit.ly/38jCnwk).

This book is designed to reminisce the lingering and seemingly ubiquitous influence of Spanish and largely American rule in the Philippines two centuries after thereabouts. It can also serve as reference material for graduate students and chiefly for professors of language and literature on account of the informative sample review papers included.

1

Linguistic Purpose & Historical Implications of Malapropism and Code-Switching in the Philippines

Michael L. Estremera
ᵃ Department of Education, Tugos Elementary School
ᵇ Sorsogon State University(SSU)
Sorsogon City 4700, Philippines
michael.estremera@deped.gov.ph

Abstract. *The present article underpins the affirmation that colonization does have historical, linguistic, and cultural impacts. Specifically, this paper explores the social malapropism and code-switching as trails of colonization dented by the American and Spanish regimes in the Philippines. The author concludes that malapropism occurs coupled with the code-switching linguistic phenomenon. Most of the malapropism episodes that transpired are a prelude to shifting from one language to another. These occurrences have veiled implications and purposes which are established by the semantic features of the discourses. Collectively, the colonizers' linguistic influence was the chief contributory factor to the preceding phenomena. Bilingualism or even multilingualism induces malapropism and code-switching occurrences inevitably. The incompetence in choosing appropriate words and the low cache of lexical terms somewhat affect the preceding phenomena. In light of the findings and conclusions, teachers must be mindful of these occurrences to cope with these phenomena accordingly, thereby converting such drawbacks to communication into rich opportunities for meaningful classroom tête-à-tête. To the extent that there is a complete communication cycle in malapropism and code-switching discourses, these could be exploited as bridges to learn the L2. Since there has likewise been language assimilation in code-switching, such can be used as an opportunity to master the* *second language by guiding learners toward fluency and accuracy. Morphological and phonological awareness will symbiotically follow sooner through series of drills and philosophical practice of the language.*

Key words*: code-switching, etymology, linguistic hegemony, multilingualism error theory, malapropism*

1. INTRODUCTION

Malapropism is an inappropriate word used inadvertently in place of another word with a related sound. Malapropisms can be comical because they give rise to irrational speeches. For instance, the common phrase "for all intents and purposes" is frequently turned into the malapropism "for all intensives and purposes." This phrase is slightly irrational, though, in this scenario, it's not comical to the extent that it is so often said mistakenly (https://cutt.ly/6es5CJs)1.

Conversely, in linguistics, code-switching or language alternation potentially transpires when a speaker substitutes between two or more languages, or language variations, in the context of a single conversation. Multilingual interlocutors of more than one language use features of multiple languages when communicating with each other.

Consequently, code-switching is the practice of more than one linguistic variability in a manner consistent with the syntax and phonology of each variety (https://cutt.ly/Hes6olH). Mukti Prabowo et al. (2018) concluded that code-switching is unavoidable as utilized in the General English classes. One major reason is that the students are not English proficient, and the lexical range is not that wide. Hence, lecturers resort to code-switching to help their students understand materials and instruction better.

The lecturer used three code-switching types in this research: tag switching, intra-sentential, and inter-sentential code-switching. However, this present research delved into code-switching as it occurred on social-media platforms and casual conversations. The interconnectedness of code-switching and malapropism occurrences had likewise been explored as there seem very few studies available highlighting the forgoing linguistic phenomena.

2. LITERATURE REVIEW

2.1 Metaphysics of Malapropism and Code-switching

There is much argument in linguistics concerning the dissimilarity between code-switching and language transfer (Treffers, 2009). In effect, the concerns of the use of code-switching as a medium of instruction in the context of English as Foreign Language (EFL) classes may have been deliberated already for many years since code-switching is deemed the last recourse used in multilingual Asians such as Indonesia (Liu, 2010; Mujiono, Poedjosoedarmo, Subroto, & Wiratno, 2013).

In some circumstances, linguists denote the benefits and disadvantages of language transfer as two separate phenomena, i.e., language transference and language interference, correspondingly (Brice, 2015). In such interpretations, these two kinds of language transfer and code-switching can encompass what is known as a cross-linguistic influence (Brice, 2015). To some degree, an instance of discourse error is called a malapropism when a word is produced that is irrational or ridiculous in context, yet similar in sound to what was intended (Fay, 1982).

Malapropisms vary from other kinds of speaking or writing errors, such as eggcorns or spoonerisms, and from the unintentional or cautious production of newly made-up words (neologisms) Zwickky, 1982). For instance, it is not a malapropism to use obtuse [wide or dull] instead of acute [narrow or sharp]; it is undoubtedly deemed a malapropism to use obtuse [stupid or slow-witted] when one means abstruse [esoteric or difficult to understand]. Malapropisms usually maintain the part of speech of the initially intended word. Similarly, substitutions tend to have the same number of syllables and metrical structure – the same form of stressed and unstressed syllables – as the envisioned word or phrase. If the stress pattern of the malapropism varies from the intended word, unstressed syllables could be deleted or inserted; stressed syllables and the collective rhythmic patterns are maintained (Sheridan, 2005).

Moreover, malapropisms, of course, are so named from Mrs. Malaprop (from the French *mal à propos,* or inappropriately), a character from Richard Sheridan's *The Rivals,* who was wont to use wrong words that occurred to sound like the ones she wanted to utter (*"He is the very pine-apple of politeness!" -> pinnacle*).

Though it's regularly regarded as stemming from ignorance, especially when politicians are making these amusing blunders, it's honestly a common communication error that can transpire even if the speaker knows the lexical definitions of the words entirely. In the same vein, we may unsurprisingly make other semantic speech mistakes, such as anticipating what we mean to say in our head and puzzlingly replacing it with its opposite. We may also substitute the word with a related word (*"Don't burn your fingers"/"Don't burn your toes"*) or in an even more perplexing use of another word that sounds like a related word (*heritage/legacy -> heresy*) (https://bit.ly/38jCnwk).

2.2 Colonization and English Language

Phillipson (1992) scrutinized the probable reasons linked to English as the world's most dominant language. He claimed that the spread of English was not unpremeditated but, in effect, carefully planned. In one of his books, he highlighted how the cultural and commercial undertakings of the colonizers played a pivotal function in determining the cultural symbol (e.g., Indian culture).

Conversely, Pennycook (1998) argues that the colonial discourse around English and English culture may have been exploited to substantiate colonial and imperial economic activities. Still, these conversations about the superiority of the former and the latter's inferiority are not common reactions of the material domain. These could have been manifestations of cultural discourse itself. To supplement, Calvet (1987) recognized two contributory steps to linguistic colonization. In Vertical step is connected to the social spread of the

English language. The European language first spread into the upper classes of the colonized people. Horizontal step, conversely, has to do with the geographical spread of language. The colonial language is diffused from the capital to the small cities and, from there, to the villages.

The colonizers mainly spend much effort through the educational system to instill this asymmetrical social ideology in their social and linguistic practices. This has likewise been underpinned by Spencer (1985), who conjectured that the colonizer's language became necessary for all those who wished to advance socially and participate in the colony's public sphere. This is true to the socially upward people who quickly eschewed the local languages and favored the colonial language. The educated increasingly opted to raise their children in a colonial language rather than an African language.

Moreover, colonization and the slave trade also led to the creation of new languages. The most well-known and studied cases are the Creole languages in European plantation societies worldwide [Carrebean, America, and Australia]. Coming from diverse social and linguistic backgrounds, their creators- such as African slaves and European indented laborers in the case of Pacific creoles (Mint & Price, 1976 and 1992).

Similarly, Holm (1989), Mufwene (2015), and Muhleisen (2010) hypothesized that due to their having emerged as a direct consequence of European slavery, their surface resemblance to the colonial language, and their encounter with populations of low reputation, Creole was held in contempt by the Europeans. They are mostly not recognized as languages in their own right but are considered make-shift languages and flawed or corrupted versions of the colonial language.

3. RESEARCH METHOD

3.1 Research Design

The author deemed qualitative research design most appropriate to capture the linguistic purpose and historical implications of code-switching and malapropism in the Philippines speech community. According to Hammarberg et al. (2016), qualitative methods are designed to investigate experience, meaning, and perspective, most often from the participant's viewpoint. The gathered data are commonly not subject to exploiting any statistical tools.

Qualitative research techniques comprise 'small-group discussions' for exploring beliefs, attitudes, and concepts of normative behavior; 'semi-structured interviews,' to seek views on a focused topic or, with key informants, for background information or an institutional perspective; 'in-depth interviews' to comprehend a condition, experience, or event from a personal standpoint; and 'analysis of texts and documents, such as government reports, media articles, websites or diaries, to learn about distributed or personal knowledge.

3.2 Participants

Participants to this undertaking are purposively selected considering the occurrences of code-switching and malapropism on social media and casual conversations. These are the social media practitioners, teachers, and students. Palinkas et al. (2013) accentuate that purposeful sampling is widely used in qualitative research to identify and select information-rich cases related to the phenomenon of interest.

Although several different purposeful sampling strategies exist, criterion sampling is most commonly used in implementation research. However, combining sampling strategies may be more appropriate to the aims of implementation research and more consistent with recent developments in quantitative methods.

3.3 Data Collection Techniques

This study primarily exploited transcription and documentary analysis as the main tool in data collection. It used textual analysis and recorded conversations to expound malapropism and code-switching as transpired over social media platforms. In effect, document analysis is a systematic procedure for reviewing or evaluating documents—both printed and electronic (computer-based and Internet-transmitted) material. Like other analytical approaches in qualitative research, document analysis necessitates that data be scrutinized and inferred to elicit meaning, gain understanding, and develop empirical knowledge (Corbin & Strauss, 2008).

4. FINDINGS

Malapropism and code-switching as trails of Spanish epoch and American regimes in the Philippines are confirmed by the preceding literature and studies in linguistics. To clarify the preceding linguistic phenomenon, the current author deems it appropriate to dichotomize and dissect the malapropism and code-switching occurrences and their concealed discourse implications and purposes accordingly. Examining the above linguistic occurrences will give rise to the etymology of the Philippines ' rich linguistic diversity.

Evident in table 1 is the occurrence of two linguistic phenomena called *malapropism* and *code-switching* committed by movie theater spectators. In the Philippines context, these occurrences seem to go together. As interlocutors attempt to transfer from one code to another, pronunciation errors or choice of words are likely to happen. The spelling of the target word is also compromised; however, its semantics aspect has also been found successful, as highlighted by the above table.

In effect, the code [**#SM&CS1**] shows a very concrete example of the above claim. The speaker started with a native language [Ay] and immediately shifted to another language [Spanish] then to another language anew [English].

Table 1: Social Malapropism & Code Switching on Movie Theater by the Spectators

CODE	DISCOURSE LINES	PHILLIPPINES CONTEXT ENGLISH TRANSLATION	LINGUISTIC PURPOSE
#SM&CS1	Ay! *Que Corny*!*I dunno* what Rock sees in her.	Oh! You're cheap! I don't know what Rock sees in her.	to express dismay/dislike
#SM&CS2	It's a *corny* love story, when you think about it.	It's a cheap love story, when you think about it.	to extend discouragement
#SM&CS3	Ay! Puede ba, you have weird taste! "She is really *cara de achay* if you ask me".	Hey! Excuse me!, you have weird taste! "She looks like a housemaid if you ask me".	to insist and discredit
#SM&CS4	She looks like a cat *aw-right*, she says with her thick, singsong accent.	She looks like a cat alright, she says with her thick, singsong accent.	to dishonor by associating offensive words
#SM&CS5	But if you ask me, prima, Gloria Talbott looks like a *trapo*.	But if you ask me, cousin, Gloria Talbott is comparable to a dish rag.	to express personal opinion
#SM&CS6	"*Pobre* Rock!" Every time he has to kiss her- Pucha shudders at the thought.	"Poor Rock!" Every time he has to kiss her – Pucha shudders at the thought.	to express mercy and sympathy

Source: *(Hagedorn, 1990)*

However, as the speaker attempts to transcode from Spanish to English, he mispronounced or even misrepresented *don't know* from *dunno*. Although the speaker here committed an error, he was able to converse successfully and was understood by the receiver of the message. Semantically, both the speaker and the receiver could complete the communication process as the receiver imbibed the implied meaning [to express dismay/dislike].

For the code [**#SM&CS2**], the speaker used a colloquial term [corny] instead of accurate lexis [cheap] to mean discouragement. This informal word has indeed been widely accepted in the Philippines archipelago when conversing. It denotes something cheap, not practical, or of low-quality material things.

To supplement, the discourse line [Ay! Puede ba, you have a weird taste! "She is really *cara de achay* if you ask me] coded as [**#SM&CS3**] reveals the lingering legacy of Spanish and American regimes in the Philippines. As noted, the speaker here is showing his multilingual prowess by using three languages [Filipino, Spanish, and English] in conversing with the receiver of the message. He started with his native language, transcoded to Spanish, and then ended his line with English lexes with the linguistic purposes of insisting and discrediting someone.

For the coded conversation [**#SM&CS4**], *malapropism* has likewise been apparent to the extent that the English word *alright* was mistakenly used as *aw-right*. However, though phonologically an error was committed, the chief purpose of communicating still transpired. The receiver of the message figured out that the speaker intends to dishonor by associating offensive words. For conversations [**#SM&CS5** and **#SM&CS6**], the linguistic phenomenon common to colonized countries is also highlighted called *code-switching*. Scrutinizing the preceding conversations fully would imply that these linguistics occurrences are closely associated with colonization.

The colonized countries, e.g., the Philippines, attempt to use the languages which a purpose in mind. The errors committed are deemed trivial for the sake of extending and expressing ideas and opinions.

To some extent, the legacy of the colonizers created a status symbol; hence, patronized and used by Filipino people in the case of the Philippines. Indeed, Spencer (1985) inferred that the colonizers' language became necessary for all those who wished to advance socially and participate in the colony's public sphere. This is true to the socially upward people who quickly eschewed the local languages and to favored the colonial language.

The educated increasingly opted to raise their children in a colonial language rather than an African language. Rafael (1993 and 1999) also discussed the interplay of *lingua franca* and the introduced language by the colonizers in the Philippines [*English and Spanish*] thru linguistic phenomena called *malapropism* and *code-switching*. The sociocultural impact was also tackled by highlighting the conversations of Filipino movie viewers watching American films.

Noteworthy, however, in the article titled *"Taglish, or the phantom power of the lingua franca"* is the occurrence of word insertions from mother tongue to either Spanish or English language, vice versa, by the interlocutors [e.g. Ay puede ba, *you have weird taste*! She's really *cara de achay* if you ask me]. The above author also established that mestizones as colonial aftermath have always been associated with the sources of power and an object of envy and perfection. This is confirmed at the outset of the article the two characters [*Rio and Pucha*] made envious descriptions of the movie actresses they viewed.

Table 2: Code Switching on Movie Theater by the Actors

CODE	DISCOURSE LINES	PHILLIPPINES CONTEXT ENGLISH TRANSLATION	LINGUISTIC PURPOSE
#SM&CS7	Edith, ano ba ang *appointments* ko *for today?*	Edith, what are appointments for today	to ask, clarify and confirm

#SM&CS8	Mamayang *five* ho, kay Mr. *Santos.* Yung *dinner* n'yo ho at seven sa bahay ng *brother* ninyo.	Later at five o'clock, to Mr. Santos. You have will have dinner in your brother's residence.	to confirm and give assurance
#SM&CS9	At saka pumirma din sa ganyang *arrangement* si Stella bago sila ikinasal ni Robbie.	Besides, Stella signed on that arrangement before they were wed with Robbie.	to insist and remind
#SM&CS10	Bakit masyado kang nagiging emotional pagdating sa dokumentong ito?	Why are you so emotional regarding this document?	to ask, clarify and confirm
#SM&CS11	*Bert, let me handle this. Hija, we are not questioning the love you have for each other. I think Phillip is a wonderful guy. He's intelligent, he's sensitive*	Bert, let me handle this. Hija, we are not questioning the love you have for each other. I think Phillip is a wonderful guy. He's intelligent, he's sensitive	to support and give opinion
#SM&CS12	*I'll make it easier for you. If Phillip doesn't sign this agreement,* at magpapakasal parin kayo, kami na ang gagalitin mo.	I'll make it easier for you. If Phillip doesn't sign this agreement, and you insist to marry him still, we'll surely get mad.	to give assurance and give warning

Source: *Taglish, or the phantom power of lingua franca by Vicente R. Rafael (p. 116-119)*

In linguistics, code-switching or language alternation transpires when a speaker replaces between two or more languages, or language variations, in the context of a single tête-à-tête. Multilingual speakers of more than one language use elements of multiple languages when communicating with each other. Accordingly, code-switching uses more than one linguistic variation in a manner consistent with the syntax and phonology of each variety (https://cutt.ly/Hes6olH). Hence, the previous table presents the occurrence of code-switching committed by the actor interlocutors. Coded dialogues [**#SM&CS7** and **#SM&CS8**] show parallelism as to linguistic purpose. Speakers here want to clarify and give assurance by using two sets of languages [English and Filipino] common to both the speaker and the listener of the message. Also, in the Philippines context, code-switching is prevalent if the speaker wishes to insist and remind the audience of impending or happening within the vicinity.

Additionally, a speaker also transcodes if he would like to support in conversation and/or give his stance in the long run on certain issues while conversing [Bert, let me handle this. Hija, we are not questioning the love you have for each other. I think Phillip is a wonderful guy. He's intelligent; he's sensitive]. In this line, the speaker sent the message by utilizing the L2 [English], followed by the Spanish word [Hija], and then back to the first code he used from the very start of the conversation. Nonetheless, for the discourse line [I'll make it easier for you. If Phillip doesn't sign this agreement, at magpapakasal pa rin kayo, kami na ang gagalitin mo.] coded as [**#SM&CS12**] confirm anew the fact that American colonization practically has had linguistic impact on the Philippines when conversing both in speech and in written form.

Table 3: Social Malapropism on Comic Plays

CODE	DISCOURSE LINES	PHILLIPPINES CONTEXT ENGLISH TRANSLATION	LINGUISTIC PURPOSE
#SM&CS7	…*bes preng* ko siya siyempre…	…he is my *best friend* that's why…	to give assurance
#SM&CS8	…*wa-is* lng ako kaya ganun…	…I am just *wise* for such…	to express practicality
#SM&CS9	…*wajawang* to know pare ha?…	…*What do you want* to know buddy huh?…	to ask and inform
#SM&CS10	…*dasbitor* kaya lng…ok sige na nga…	…*That is better*, but,…ok I agree…	to agree
#SM&CS11	…mas ok ng maging *jeprox* para in sa grupo…	…Being *hippie* is ok to be with the group's fashion…	to express practicality
#SM&CS12	…haha..loko ka talaga...anong *say mo* dun..ok ba?…	…haha…you're such fool buddy…*What do you say to that?*…is it nice?…	to ask for opinion
#SM&CS13	…*we-no?!*..wala kang pakialam dun ok?..	…Oh, well, so what?...none of your business ok?…	to insist

***Source:** (Marcelo, 1987)*

A linguistic phenomenon termed malapropism is an unfitting word used unintentionally in place of another word with a similar sound. Malapropisms can be funny-sounding since they give rise to illogical statements. For example, the common phrase "for all intents and purposes" is often turned into the malapropism "for all intensives and purposes." This phrase is slightly irrational, though in this case, it's not funny at all because, at times, it is also said erroneously by some speakers (https://cutt.ly/6es5CJs).

Table 3 confirms that malapropism as an aftermath of colonization varies from country to country and race to race. However, despite the noted phonologic and morphologic error, the user's language identity where malapropism happened still carries its linguistic identity. Semantically, speakers and receivers of the information can still deduce between and beyond the lines of communication.

The main purposes of conversation still transpired, as highlighted by the preceding table of malapropism occurrence on comic plays. Coded discourse lines such as [**#SM&CS7, #SM&CS8, #SM&CS9, #SM&CS10, #SM&CS11, #SM&CS12,** and **#SM&CS13**] are a concrete example of malapropism due to American colonization. Filipinos during those times nativized or even invented queer words or languages by combining the native language and the English language in comic plays. These comic plays are reading materials that depict the Philippines' hot issues and concerns during those times.

However, some patriotic persons denounce this linguistic phenomenon as it distorts the original word. However, if investigated carefully, the lexes form meaning and have concealed linguistic purposes.

Table 4: Code-Switching on Broadcast Media

CODE	DISCOURSE LINES	PHILLIPPINES CONTEXT ENGLISH TRANSLATION	LINGUISTIC PURPOSE
#SM&CS14	Si *Bong Lopez will be giving us the details of this activity that will happen today* urog nang gayo dara kan *RJE Production.*	Bong Lopez will be giving us the details of this activity that will happen today brought to us by the RJE Production.	to notify
#SM&CS15	*Now,* sisay naman ang nakaantabay sa ciudad nin Sorsogon…*because* an *major thoroughfares* iyo po tabi…ang magiging *venue*…	Now, whoever is tuning in us in the city of Sorsogon…because the major thoroughfares will be the venue.	to clarify and guide
#SM&CS16	Ngonyan na aga… nuh…*while we will not be able to cover live..but of course* nakalibot po diyan an ating mga *reporters.*	This morning, nuh… while we will not be able to cover live..but of course reporters are at the venue to monitor.	to give assurance
#SM&CS17	Si Jerry Bigtas mga kababayan… sigurado yadi ine sa *contingent* kan Casiguran...	Jerry will surely be joining in Casiguran contingent.	to express certainty
#SM&CS18	So...may *possibility* din *that Mar Romero will be in the delegation of Pilar or Donsol area.*	So… there is also a possibility that Mar Romero will be in the delegation of Pilar or Donsol area.	to conclude

#SM&CS19	Then, alas *nuebe nin aga ngonyan, iyo po an Historico de Culural Parrade.*	Then, at nine o'clock will be History of Cultural Parrade.	to supplement
#SM&CS20	Buenas dias es todos mis amigos es mis amigas, cumadres es cumpadres …senyores, senyoritas de las familias… It's specially working holiday nuh… for the province of Sorsogon.	Good day to you everyone, my friends, ladies, gentlemen, buddies and the members of the family. It's a specially working holiday nuh… for the province of Sorsogon.	to express positivity and to inform
#SM&CS21	*In celebration of our Kasanggayanhan Festival*..iyo man talaga an ano… an…*culminating activity…*	In celebration of our Kasanggayanhan Festival..this is really the… the…culminating activity…	to reminisce
#SM&CS22	*And then we have the Sorsogon thanks giving day..and a mass in celebration for the 125th founding anniversary…* ine an ahhh…*activity* natin…	And then we have the Sorsogon thanks giving day..and a mass in celebration for the 125th founding anniversary… this is the…ahhh..our activity…	to notify
#SM&CS23	*Okay?...that will be today*..kaya naka "Kasanggayan" *t-shirt* ako ngayon…yang ang	Okay?...that will be today..that's why I am wearing a "*Prosperity*" t-shirt today…this is the t-	to express jubilation

	t-shirt ng Sangguniang Panlalawigan	shirt of Provincial Board Members	
#SM&CS24	So mga darling, mga sweetheart, mga mahal, bago an gabos, sana giyahan kita sa aldaw ine…taw-an kita ki maray na lawas asin salud.	At this point, honey, sweetheart, love, before anything else, let us pray for a strong body anda good health for all.	to spread positive vibes
#SM&CS25	*Oh huh…harayuon pa ine..this is swimsuit competition ...*	*Oh huh…this is still far…this is swimsuit competition..*	to anticipate

Source: *Padaba Radio Live Simulcast, October 17, 2019.*

Broadcast media are undoubtedly powerful instruments of spreading information regarding debatable issues and concerns. *Taglish* (combination of Tagalog and English language) became the preferred idiom of popular dissent, especially in the period following the assassination of Benigno "Ninoy" Aquino (popular politician) in 1983, culminating in the People Power Revolt of 1986. Urban discourse critical of the Marcoses [Filipino Dictator President] took the form of puns, jokes, and assorted wordplay on the regime's pronouncements and the names of its leaders (Rafael, 1986).

Thus, to confirm whether such manifestations of code-switching have still prospered to the present date or not, table 4 below has been made intently for this purpose. It is noticeable that broadcast media still practice code-switching from mother tongue to the national language and English, or Filipino and English language only with linguistic purposes to convey messages to the audience effectively. Codes [**#SM&CS14** and **#SM&CS15**] are meant to notify, clarify, and guide the listeners of the event within the speech community. Speaker started by using the Filipino word [Si] and immediately shifted to English lexes [Bong Lopez will be giving us the details of this activity that will happen today] and ended his discourse through a known dialect to the radio hearers [urog ng gayo]. To further establish the occurrence of code-switching, the discourse line [Ngonyan na aga... nuh...while we will not be able to cover live..but of course nakalibot po diyan an ating mga] involves the use of Bicol dialect (one of the Philippine languages), and English lexes with conjunction, pronoun, modal, verb, and a noun; however, it ended with the use Bicol of dialects.

This sudden shift from one language to another practically confirms that the Filipinos still embrace English as one of the legacies of American colonization in this modern and technological epoch. Moreover, the coded speech line as [#**SM&CS20**] also confirms that the Spanish colonization has also been successful in their mission to spread their language identity. The speaker threw some Spanish lexes [Buenas dias es todos mis amigos es mis amigas, cumadres es cumpadres ...senyores, senyoritas de las familias] in form of greetings and ended his line by using English words.

In this line, the speaker's purpose could probably be deduced from the cultural background of the Filipinos. In a nutshell, the preceding speech lines are designed to express positivity and set the speaker's tone. For the code [#**SM&CS21**], the speaker used the English language and Bicol dialect to reminisce the scheduled events, informing the listeners of the nearing events.

Linguistically, this odd combination of two languages may appear erroneous; but, in the context of the listeners and the speaker, they had been able to reach the common point of communication. This could be so due to the familiarity of both the speaker and the audiences of two or three languages.

Table 5: Malapropism during Casual Conversations by the Millennial High School Students

CODE	DISCOURSE LINES	PHILLIPPINES CONTEXT ENGLISH TRANSLATION	LINGUISTIC PURPOSE

#SM&CS26	*Bruh…let's trip*	Let us go… brother	to order
#SM&CS27	*You are parking at the wrong gate…hahaha..sabi ng friend ko but actually it should be…*	You are barking at the wrong tree…hahaha..my friend told me… but actually it should be…	to evoke argument
#SM&CS28	Hoy..*please pick up the paper* naman *and fall it in the trash can…*	Hey..please pick up the paper and throw it in the trash can…	to give a command
#SM&CS29	Sir… our principal is *revolving* around the corridor now.	Sir… our principal is walking around the corridor now.	to notify and warn
#SM&CS30	Hello… please open window—let the *airforce* come in.	Hello… please open window—let the air come in.	to request and insist

Source 1: *Ben P. Lacay, High School English Teacher (October 17, 2019)*
Source 2: *Maclette Villapando, Senior High School English Teacher (October 17, 2019)*
Source 3: *Cyril Victoria, IELTS Coach (October 17, 2019)*

In the Philippines, with very rich linguistic typologies, malapropism occurs inevitably coupled with code-switching as well. Offenders usually try to shift from one code to another, from native to the English language, in particular. They find it difficult to think of the most appropriate word; hence, similarly-sounding words are usually substituted to complete the sentence and send the message successfully.

For instance, [*Bruh…let's trip*] translated into English as "Let's go brother" means that the speaker abbreviated the word brother for simply "bro." However, "bruh" and "bro" differ phonologically. The former lexis perhaps is influenced by mother-tongue accent while the latter of course is more appropriate. In fact, the former has been widely used in the Bicol archipelago to address someone [a close friend, male stranger, or more often than not, referring to a brother itself].

As for the words "trip" and "go," where the former was mistakenly used, it denotes that the speaker associated the foregoing word to the strolling, which somehow is relevant to the word "go" semantically. Be that as it may, the receiver of the message surpassed these barriers to communication; hence, the purpose of the communication was still achieved. In addition, the speech line [*You are parking at the wrong gate*…hahaha..sabi ng friend ko but actually it should be...] coded as [**#SM&CS27**] was inaccurately used instead of "You are barking at the wrong tree." The speaker here erroneously used the word "*parking*" instead of "*barking*" due per chance to the phonological similarity of the words. Moreover, the word "gate" was likewise used instead of the most appropriate word, "tree" to complete the message. Though the words "gate" and "tree" are not related in meaning, the speaker perhaps opted to use the wrong word to associate to the word "parking."

Figuratively, the implied meaning could not be understood by the receiver of the message; unless the said sentence means another meaning known to both the sender and the receiver of the text. Apparent in code [**#SM&CS28**] is the misappropriate use of the semantically related lexes "*fall*" and "*throw*" in the Philippines context and perchance to other countries with English as a second language (L2). The sender of the text used the word "*fall*" instead of "*throw*" to complete the communication process.

These verbs both imply a command action to be done by the receiver of the message. The chief reason for this linguistic occurrence is the inability of the speaker to determine their appropriate grammatical usage and functions to come up with proper sentences. Low vocabulary power could also be one of the reasons for malapropism in the above case. In like manner, the discourse line [*Sir… our principal is revolving around the corridor now.*] with assigned code [**#SM&CS29**] likewise shows a clear occurrence of malapropism committed by the high school millennial students as shared by their respective teachers. As noted, the sender of the message used the word "revolving" instead of the accurate word "walking." Possibly, the speaker somehow was able to send the message and was construed by the teacher as the receiver of the message. This could be so since the parts of speech [noun] used in the above conversation are the same insofar as the exact word is concerned; hence, the meaning was still established. In the long run, in code [**#SM&CS30**], the word *"airforce"* in the request sentence "Hello... please open window—let the airforce come in." was interchangeably used with simply *"air"* to come up with a correct sentence.

The reason for this could also be phonological anew. Social media are interactive computer-mediated technologies that facilitate creating and sharing information, ideas, career interests, and other forms of expression via virtual communities and networks. The variety of stand-alone and built-in social media services currently available introduces challenges of definition; however, there are some common features: (i) social media are interactive Web 2.0 Internet-based applications; (ii) user-generated content, such as text posts or comments, digital photos or videos, and data generated through all online interactions, is the lifeblood of social media; and, (iii) users create service-specific profiles and identities for the website or app that are designed and maintained by the social media organization.

Social media facilitate the development of online social networks by connecting a user's profile with those of other individuals or groups (Obar et al., 2015, and Ellison, 2007).

Figure 1: Malapropism on Social Media

Source: Ben P. Lacay High School English Teacher (October 17, 2019)

As for figure 1, B, the dialogue starts with " Ikaw na lang pa tattoo pre, inom na lang ako ng mineral" translated as [*You better be the one trying the tattoo buddy, I'd rather drink a mineral water*]. This is followed up by a sentence in Filipino " Pa tattoo tayo pre." The receiver of information also replied in Filipino "Saan" equivalent to [*where*] in English.

The sender then said, " Sa dibdib, yong XXII, yong roman mineral," translated as [*Near the chest, the XXII, the roman numerals*]. Dichotomizing the conversation implies that the word *mineral* was used to mean *numerals*. The sender of the text may not recall the right word; hence, he opted to use erroneously *mineral* to complete the communication sequence. Relative to the last figure (1.C), the sentence [At the end of the day, we are human beans] has likewise been a manifestation of malapropism occurrence on social media. The word *"Beans"* was used mistakenly instead of *beings* which sounded similar to the former lexis.

5. DISCUSSION

As accentuated by Gumperz (1982), Poplack et al. (1982), and Muysken (1995), code-switching still has semantic features in conveying messages. Communication is still possible despite the noted errors in the delivery of the message. In malapropism also, on account of its negative image and comical value, the sender of information can still deliver what is supposed to be conveyed. Hence, it is but proper to emphasize that these linguistic phenomena should unveil its positive aspect for the sake of communication.

The goal must always be understanding the text, and errors along the communication channels must have been deemed negligible and trivial. It should open the door of acceptance and reverence due to cultural differences and linguistic typologies. Based on the results and conclusion, teachers must be aware of these linguistic episodes to cope with these phenomena accordingly. To the extent that there is a complete communication cycle in malapropism and code-switching occurrences, this could be used to bridge learning the L2. Since there has also been language assimilation in code-switching, this can be used as an avenue to master the second language by guiding learners toward fluency and accuracy of the target language. Learning of structure will just follow through series of drills and good practice.

Moreover, as underscored by Phillipson (1992), Pennycook (1998), Calvet (1987), Spencer (1995), Holm (1989), and Mufwene (1997), the spread of the English language was due to cultural and economic activities of the colonizers. Moreover, they likewise conjectured that the colonial discourse around English and English culture may have been employed to justify colonial and imperial economic activities, but these conversational about the superiority of the former and the inferiority of the latter are not mere reflexes of the material domain. These could have been manifestations of cultural discourse itself. The present paper confirms that the spread of the English language in the Philippines is chiefly due to American colonization. It continues to thrive even up to the current digital era. The English language created a status symbol putting a demarcation line between English-proficient and non-proficient Filipinos. The practice of code-switching [*Filipino to English generally*] is a manifestation of cultural and linguistic hegemony. English-speaking Filipinos still earn the top spot in media, entertainment, politics, and education. In the long run, this paper also highlights that, historically, the Spanish regime also contributed to the linguistic typology of the Philippines. The discourse lines [table 4] on broadcast media, in particular, indicate linguistic dominion by the Spaniards in the Philippines. The Spanish language is still found in some educational materials and literary plays of the Philippines to date.

6. Conclusion

Figure 2: Interplay of Malapropism and Code-switching

The studies conducted by Gumperz (1982), Poplack et al. (1982), and Muysken (1995) primarily delved into the lexical and semantic effect of code-switching in discourse. On the other hand, Fay (1982), Zwisly (1982), and Aitchinson (2012) investigated the phonological aspect of malapropism occurrence. It is, therefore, worthy to note that the previous scholars explored code-switching and malapropism in the context of monolingualism. This could imply that they conducted investigations of such phenomena in an English-speaking country with English as the language of the majority. None of these linguists scrutinized the occurrence of malapropism and code-switching in a multilingual milieu simultaneously. This research vacuum was filled-in the by the current research venture. Thus, figure 2 delineates the interplay of malapropism and code-switching in the Philippines to complete the communication process. Based on the previous discussion, the present author concluded that malapropism occurs in the Philippines coupled with the code-switching linguistic phenomenon. Most of the malapropism episodes that transpired are indeed prerequisites to shifting from one code to another.

These linguistic episodes have veiled linguistic purposes, which are manifested by the semantic elements of the dialogues. The cultural influence dented by the colonizers like American and Spanish is the chief contributory factor to the preceding linguistic phenomena. Filipinos try to be bilingual or multilingual both in spoken and written ways where errors are likely to happen. The inability to choose or low cache of vocabulary words could be slightly one reason behind the phenomena. Carefully scrutinizing the above inferences led to the language theory formulation relative to the interplay of code-switching and malapropism occurrence in multilingual countries called **Multilingualism Error Theory**.

The Philippines has rich linguistic typologies with over a hundred languages and dialectal variations apart from English as a second language (L2). The exposure of the interlocutors to diverse variations of languages is the major reason for such phenomena. Speakers tend to barrow, insert, transcode, and invent new lexes either accidentally or intentionally; thus, the occurrence of malapropism and code-switching inevitably transpire. As they converse, errors in pronunciation and morphology are at times risked. However, these errors do not hamper the communication cycle. Both the sender and the receiver of the message reach the common point of discourse. This theory also explains that mistakes committed by multilingual speakers in communication are subject to second thought.

This means that offenders of malapropism and code-switching could also be aware of the appropriate word to insert; however, there may be some factors behind the commission of errors such as inhibition, internal and external disturbances, personal reasons, a stockpile of lexical terms, phonological and morphological differences and similarities of the languages being used in discourses. The sophistication brought by code-switching and the entertainment value of social malapropism in the research locale, in particular, could also be one of the many factors.

REFERENCES

Brice, A.E. (2015). *"Multilingual Language Development."* International Encyclopedia of the Social & Behavioral Sciences. 2: 57–64. doi:10.1016/B978-0-08-097086-8.23126-7. ISBN 9780080970875. Retrieved from https://cutt.ly/4edpaUZ. October 17, 2019.

Calvet, Louis-Jean. (1987). *La guerre des langues et les politiques linguistiques*, Paris: Payot. (English version: *Language wars and linguistic politics*. tr. by Michel Petheram. Oxford and New York: Oxford University Press, 1998.)

Corbin, J. & Strauss, A. (2008). Basics of qualitative research: Techniques and procedures for developing grounded theory (3rd ed.). Thousand Oaks, CA: Sage.

Cromdal, Jakob (2001). *"Overlap in Bilingual Play: Some Implications of Code-Switching for*

Febiyaska, E. A., Ardi, P. (2019). *Indonesian-English Code-Switching in Gogirl! Magazine: Types and Features.* JELTL (Journal of English Language Teaching and Linguistics). e-ISSN: 2502-6062, p-ISSN: 2503-1848, Vol. 4(3) www.jeltl.org.

Fay, David; Cutler, Anne (1977). *"Malapropisms and the Structure of the Mental Lexicon".* Linguistic Inquiry. 8 (3): 505–520. JSTOR 4177997. Retrieved from https://cutt.ly/eedpLX9. October 17, 2019.

Gumperz, J. (1982). *Discourse Strategies.* Cambridge: Cambridge University Press.

John, Holm (1989). *Pidgins and creoles.* Volume II. Reference survey. Cambridge: Cambridge University Press, 1989. Pp. xxv + 445, 11 maps. Retrieved from https://bit.ly/3lg0pO3. March 12, 2021.

Liu, Jingxia (2010). *Teachers' Code-Switching to the L1 in EFL Classroom.* The Open Applied Linguistics Journal, 2010, 3, 10-23.

Mint & Price (1992). *The Miracle of Creolization: A Retrospective.* New West Indian Guide, volume 75 number 1 & 2 (2001): 35-64. Retrieved from https://bit.ly/3cmXeA5. March 12, 2021.

Mufwene, S.S., (2015). *Pidgin and Creole Languages.* International Encyclopedia of the Social & Behavioral Sciences,2nd edition, Vol 18. Oxford: Elsevier. pp. 133–145.ISBN: 9780080970868. Retrieved from

Mujiono, Poedjosoedarmo, S., Subroto, E., & Wiratno, T. (2013). *Code switching in English as foreign language instruction practiced by the English lecturers at universities.* International Journal of Linguistics, 5(2), 46.

Muhleisen, Susanne (2010). *Heterogeneity in Word-Formation Patterns.* John Benjamins Publishing Company, 2010. ISBN: 978--90-272-0585-8, Prix: 95 €, 245 pages. https://doi.org/10.4000/lexis.1791.

Mukti, Prabowo, W. T & Ena, T. O. (2018). *The Use of Code Switching in General English Classes for Non-English Department Students in Indonesia.* Indonesian Journal of EFL and Linguistics. Vol. 3 No. 2, eISSN: 2503-4197, pISSN: 2527-5070 www. indonesian-efl-journal.org.

Muysken, Pieter (1995). *"Code-switching and grammatical theory".* In L. Milroy; P. Muysken (eds.). One Speaker, Two Languages: Cross-disciplinary Perspectives on Code-switching. Cambridge: Cambridge University Press. pp. 177–98. Retrieved from https://cutt.ly/iedyHOj. October 21, 2019.

Lawrence A Palinkas, L. A., Horwitz, S. M., Green C. A., Wisdom J. P. (2013). *Purposeful Sampling for Qualitative Data Collection and Analysis in Mixed Method Implementation Research.* Administration and Policy in Mental Health and Mental Health Services Research 42(5). DOI: 10.1007/s10488-013-0528-y.

Pennycook (1998). *English and the Discourses of Colonialism.* London: Routledge. ISBN: 0-415-17847-9 (hardback); 0-415-17848-7 (paperback). pp.256. https://doi.org/10.1177%2F13670069010050010702.

Phillipson, C. (1982) *Capitalism and the Construction of Old Age.* London: Macmillan. Retrieved from https://bit.ly/30CY85X. March 12, 2021.

Poplack, Shana; David Sankoff (1982). *"Borrowing: the synchrony of integration".* Linguistics. 22 (269): 99–136. doi:10.1515/ling.1984.22.1.99. hdl:10315/2840.

Sheridan, Richard Brinsley (2008). The Rivals: A Comedy, retrieved2012-07-10"Quotations from Richard Brinsley Sheridan". Poem Hunter. Retrieved 2012-07-10. There are not alligators on the banks of the Nile, although there are crocodiles. Retrieved from https://cutt.ly/Redp0G4. October 17, 2019.

Spencer, S. G. (1995). *Technical note: Video-based three-dimensional morphometrics.* American Journal of Physical Anthropology 96:443-453. https://doi.org/10.1002/ajpa.1330960409.

Treffers, J. (2009). *Language Dominance and Lexical Diversity: How Bilinguals and L2 Learners Differ in their Knowledge and Use of French Lexical and Functional Items.* University of Reading. Retrieved from https://bit.ly/3rSjiJD. March 12, 2021.

Zwicky, Arnold (1982). *"Classical malapropisms and the creation of the mental lexicon".* In Loraine Obler and Lise Menn (ed.). Exceptional Language and Linguistics(PDF). Academic Press. pp. 115–132. ISBN 978-0-12-523680-5. Retrieved 2013-09-12. Retrieved from https://cutt.ly/IedpX6B. October 17, 2019.

2

Malapropism and Code Switching as Literary Devices in Original Filipino Rap Music

Synopsis: *The Philippines was a colony of the United States from 1898 to 1946. American culture had a profound impact on the country, influencing its government, education, social institutions, language, and music. (Schons, 2010). Disco, Funk, and Motown soul music, popular on American military bases, found their way onto local radio stations in the Philippines. Rap music was introduced in the country during the 1980s and flourished during the 1990s (Onemusicph, 2016). Dichotomizing the apparent use of malapropism and code-switching is consistently used in lyrical rap content in the Philippines. As rap music in the accentuated Southeast Asian country continues to evolve, literary devices such as code-switching and malapropism are existent as methods in the lyrical pen game. Local rap artists such as Gloc-9, Ex-Battalion, Loonie, Andrew E., Salbakuta, EZ Mil, and Francis Magalona devised code-switching and malapropism in their respective lyrical compositions. Code-switching and malapropism, in general, are reputed to be grammatically rudimentary. Malapropism and code-switching can be beneficial literary devices to present a more entertaining and creative contemporary piece of literature in a literary approach. In the current Original Pilipino Music (OPM) scene, code-switching and malapropism are considered creative devices to channel lyrical content's artistic premise and descriptive layout. The presence of these particular literary devices likewise demonstrates the scope of influence of colonialism and globalization in the creative endeavors of Filipinos. In retrospect, it can be settled that like language, music, and* *literary expressions adapt as influences, whether intended or forced, come as apparent in language and culture.*

1. INTRODUCTION

Dissecting the evident use of malapropism and code-switching is consistently used in lyrical rap content in the Philippines. As rap music in the underscored Southeast Asian country evolves, literary devices such as code-switching and malapropism are extant as techniques in the lyrical pen game. Local rap artists such as Gloc-9, Ex- Battalion, Loonie, Andrew E., Salbakuta, EZ Mil, and Francis Magalona devised code-switching and malapropism in their respective lyrical compositions.

Such devices and usage can be traced to the history of colonialism in the Philippines (Estremera, 2021). Also noting that rap music is a by-product of expatriate influences, Estremera's study on linguistic purpose and historical implications of such devices in Filipino culture attaches. His study also coined malapropism as an inappropriate word used unintentionally in place of another word with a related sound. Also described in the study was the operative definition of code-switching. Code-switching, in its operative state, is the practice of more than one linguistic variability in a manner consistent with the syntax and phonology of each variety. These devices are part of the common elements of rap music. (Vicencio, 2011).

In investigating the usage of malapropism and code-switching in rap music, lyrical rap is a literary expression accompanied by beats and, or, music. Such expression creates an entertaining interplay between words, sound, and descriptive narratives.

One such example of malapropism as a technique in rap composition can be heard in EZ Mil's song, The Slashy Show:

"I could be a rap magazine
Where you look for metaphors
I might be The Source…"

(Miller, 2020)

Notice the last two words in the third line. The term 'the source' can also be mistaken as 'thesaurus,' particularly when rapped. The term 'thesaurus' also supports the illustration presented in the first two lines of the stanza. In rap terminology, the rapper also caused a *'double entendre.'*

Code-switching is also evident in Pilipino rap music. The Philippines' main influencer in rap music is Francis Magalona, device code-switching numerously in his tracks. One such example appears in his rap song 'Man From Manila':

"Tayo'y mga alipin sa sariling lupain. Tinamnan ng ninuno. Perlas ng Silanganan.

Inararo ang likas na mayamang Pilipinas. Mindanao, Visayas at Luzon.

I'm ready to defend the 3 stars and the sun. Manila ang sabi ng iba ay Maynila.

Tayo'y isinilang para upang di maging alila ng kahit nino mang sino mang dayuhan..."

(Magalona, 1990)

In the third line of the stanza, it can be perceived that the language switched from Filipino to English, then swiftly changed to Filipino once more. This phenomenon is common and often articulated in Pilipino rap songs.

This paper suggests the existence of malapropism and code-switching in a significant sub-culture in the Philippines. Discussions in this paper are referenced from articles, studies, and other noteworthy materials that reflect the social and historical context of the title.

2. DISCUSSION

2.1 History of Rap Music in the Philippines

The Philippines was a colony of the United States from 1898 to 1946. American culture had a profound impact on the country, influencing its government, education, social institutions, language, and music. (Schons, 2010). Disco, Funk, and Motown soul music, popular on American military bases, found their way onto local radio stations in the Philippines. Rap music was introduced in the country during the 1980s and flourished during the 1990s (Onemusicph, 2016). In Estremera's (2021) discussion, the historical implications of malapropism and code-switching are evident in the language of the Philippines. Colonization played a significant role in the occurrence, which is also apparent and taught in the emergence of the rap culture in the country.

2.2 Code-Switching as an Accepted Element in Filipino Rap Lyrics

Filipino rappers put together their lyrics with Filipino, English, Spanish, and even Chinese language. As this is evident in Filipino culture, the acquired influences in different languages, with a significant history of colonialism in the country, permit the writer to switch between other languages unconsciously. It is not because of a deficiency of language ability but as an acceptable result of language acquisition (Wei, 2006).

An example can be extracted from the rap song 'Yearly':

"Markang iiwanan ay masasabi na mala- sapok ni Joe Frazier (Yow, haymaker!)
Mayabang mang sabihin pero kami 'yong kahulugan ng salitang hitmaker,
'Di matatanggi, malabong mabura, gamitin sangkatutak na eraser,
Rest, stay there. 'Wag niyo nang pilitin lumabas kami bilang diss- maker."

(Ex Battalion, 2021)

Another pattern is evident in the song 'S2pid Luv':

"...mahilig kang manguleksyon binalewala aking attention

Yo, anyway, everyday iba't ibang guys ang iyong ka text and then one time nahuli kita na mayroon kang sex mas gugustuhin ko pa na magpa-crucify

Kes harap-harapan mo akong stupify so don't be mad, so don't be sad lahat ng kabulukan mo'y ilalahad."

(Salbakuta, 2002)

2.3 Malapropism as an Ancient Literary Technique

One of the most famous writers who devised malapropism to deliver stories comically is William Shakespeare. (Coruna, 2001) Coruna states that although Shakespeare had used the literary device of malapropism for comic effect, the term derives from Richard Brinsley Sheridan's character Mrs. Malaprop in his play The Rivals (1775); her name is taken from the French word "malapropos" (' inappropriate") and is typical of Sheridan's practice of concocting names to indicate the essence of a character.

2.4 Malapropism as an Intentional Creative Device

It may come as ironic that malapropism can be intentional. But in literary expressions, calculated inappropriateness can emphasize and give the reader or listener more entertainment. Such is inherent in EZ Mil's Act 1 album. The album's tracks contain themes and literary techniques that are considered unconventional in most mainstream rap songs. One style stands out in EZ Mil's tracks. His pen game consists of triple and double extenders, which are often created when he devises malapropism.

An example can be seen in EZ Mil's track 'IDK' (2020):

"With fear grabbin iron
Man, so
Marvel over the way I
Diss... dis-r-e-s-p-e-c-t-bone crushin
A rib when I drive a stake thru the heart of
A busted body kit
(Vroom vroom!)
Of a rusted Dodge 'n drift
That muscle modded shit So fuck it while-we-get...
RECCT like 'r'-e-c-t-mobile!"

3. CONCLUSION

Code-switching and malapropism, in general, are reputed to be grammatically rudimentary. In a literary approach, however, malapropism and code-switching can be useful literary devices to present a more entertaining and creative contemporary piece of literature. In the current Original Pilipino Music (OPM) scene, code-switching and malapropism are considered innovative devices to channel lyrical content's artistic premise and descriptive layout. The existence of these particular literary devices also proves the scope of influence of colonialism and globalization in the creative endeavors of Filipinos. In retrospect, it can be settled that like language, music, and literary expressions adapt as influences, whether intended or forced, come as apparent in language and culture.

REFERENCES

Antonio, D. (2016). Five remarkable rap artists in the Philippines https://www.onemusic.ph/news/5-remarkable-rap-artists-in-the-philippines Bradley, A. (2009). Book of rhymes: the poetics of hip hop . New York:

Basic Civitas, 23. Coruna, L. (2001). Shakespeare's use of malapropisms and their translation into Spanish, https://rua.ua.es/dspace/bitstream/10045/5323/1/RAEI_14_16.pdf

Estremera, M. L. (2021). Linguistic purpose and historical implications of malapropism and code-switching in the Philippines. Indonesian Journal of EFL and Linguistics, 6(1), 169. https://doi.org/10.21462/ijefl.v6i1.353

Ex Battalion (Artist). (2021). Yearly (Song). Ex Battalion Entertainment.

Magalona, Francis (Artist). (1990). Man From Manila (Song). OctoArts International.

Mayers, T. (2014). Rap wordplay and its used literary devices. The Source, 13. Retrieved: https://genius.com/Rap-genius-glossary-of-literary-devices-and-forms-ofwordplay-used-in-hip-hop-lyrics

Miller, Ezekiel (Artist). (2020). IDK (Song). FFP Records.

Miller, Ezekiel (Artist). (2020). The Slashy Show (Song). FFP Records.

Salbakuta (Artist).(2002). S2pidLuv (Song). Neo Records. Vicencio, C (2011, February 8). "The Evolution of HipHop." https://prezi.com/ml4x9xjahcz3/the-evolution-of-hip-hop-in-the-philippines.

Wei, M. (2006). Code-switching as a result of language acquisition. Language Journal, 17. https://files.eric.ed.gov/fulltext/ED564116

3

Malapropism, Code-switching in Philippine Context and American Literature Perspective

Synopsis: *This review paper presents a discussion on Code-switching and Malapropism, likewise highlighted on the research study conducted by Dr. Michael L. Estremera titled "Linguistic Purpose and Historical Implications of Malapropism and Code-switching in the Philippines." This also tries to link malapropism and code-switching in the Philippine context and to American literature. Further, the author of this paper uses contextualized material to provide examples of existing code-switching in the Philippines, Taglish, and how it is used in Philippine entertainment and socialization. On the other hand, the author also cites an excerpt from William Shakespeare's play, Romeo and Juliet, to verify the writer's claim that malapropism exists in Western literature's work. With the help of reliable references, this paper was realized. The author has gained a wider understanding despite code-switching and malapropism being used differently from a code's universal and standard function; these two (2) contribute to sociolinguistic aspects and literature.*

To conclude, If English is a language and a medium of communication, there's a need for people living in English-speaking countries to be fluent or at least be familiar with the code to live. But if a group of people lives in a non-English-speaking country, there's probably no need to study and master English. Thus, it doesn't mean people who can't talk straight English has lower IQ than those who can since English is simply one of the mediums to communicate; it's just all about a matter of surviving.

1. INTRODUCTION

Language is the principal method of human interaction, and every language in every nation is being used based on one's personal, social, work-related, and other purposes. But the main function of a language is to communicate. In sociolinguistics, a language may be referred to as a code. A code is a neutral term that can denote a language or a variety of languages (https://www.ello.uos.de). The term "code" means the target language being used by the speaker, native or not.

Further, code-switching is mostly used within bilingual and multilingual communities, and there are many reasons to use this method, such as the need to fit in with a group, as a force of habit, or to convey thoughts and concepts that might be easier to explain in a specific language (https://www.unitedlanguagegroup.com). For instance, *"Sometimes I'll start a sentence in English y termino en Español* (McArthur, 2005). In the given sample statement, the former's code is English, and the latter's in Spanish, which means 'and finish it in English.'

This linguistic phenomenon is called hybridization due to mixed elements from two codes or languages used within each sentence or clause. The other type of code-switching is intra- sentential code-switching or code-mixing. For example, *"This morning I hantar my baby tu dekat babysitter tu lah,"* it means *'This morning I took my baby to the babysitter'* (Romaine, 2000:55). The speaker switches between two codes which are Malay and English, within the phrases and clauses.

The given definition and examples of code-switching provide deep and thorough gist on how and why all races and ethnicities possibly do it; indeed, it exists across the globe. It helps every speaker to easily communicate whatever purposes they have in mind in applying and practicing code-switching.

On the other hand, aside from code-switching, one of the important concepts in this reflection paper is a malapropism.

Malapropisms are incorrect words used in place of correct words; these can be unintentional or intentional, but both cases have a comedic effect. For instance, *"The doctor administered the anecdote."* The doctor is meant to administer an "antidote," or remedy, rather than an "anecdote," or story (https://literaryterms.net).

How malapropism is unintentionally or intentionally used in any discourse should be courteously corrected and not tolerated nor laughed at, especially if the speaker is not a native of the target language. Inevitably, even the native speaker of a specific language may wrongly choose a lexicon due to the similarity of the sounds of some words like in the example, 'anecdote' and 'antidote.'

These code-switching and malapropism do exist in the Philippines, and it's ubiquitous since the country has 8 (eight) major dialects: Bikol, Cebuano, Hiligaynon (Ilonggo), Ilocano, Kapampangan, Pangasinan, Tagalog, and Waray and more than 170 language varieties across the country (https://www.marstranslation.com). In addition, the Philippines has a population of over 85 million. Indeed, not to uplift the linguistic competence of Filipinos, but having this number of different dialects, they can be considered multilingual speakers, not just bilingual.

The same scenario is applied to any literary works. Some writers consciously or unconsciously use code-switching and even malapropism in their works to add drama, humor or let the reader dig deeper into the text to get its underlying meaning. Thus, one of the goals of this paper is to look for some code-switching and malapropism in any instances in the Philippine setting and American literature work and perspectives.

2. DISCUSSION

Estremera (2021) pointed out that the exposure of the interlocutors to diverse languages is the principal reason for such phenomena. Speakers tend to barrow, insert, transcode, and invent new lexes either accidentally or intentionally; thus, the occurrence of malapropism and code-switching inevitably transpire. As they converse, errors in pronunciation and morphology are at times risked. However, these errors do not hamper the communication cycle. Both the sender and the receiver of the message reach the common point of discourse. The abovementioned researcher's claim is supported by Gumperz (1983), who gives the idea that code-switching could be seen as a real, specific discourse strategy for bilinguals. He calls code-switching code-alternation. It can occur in a quotation when the speaker directly uses a piece of reported speech in the produced language. In the case of addressee specification, the switch of language is merely used to direct the message to one of the possible addressees.

On the other hand, bilingual speakers tend to use code-switching for interjections or simple sentence fillers. Code-switching occurs when speakers know two distinct varieties and can keep them apart, although they may not do so habitually. Code-switching is a controllable strategy, differing from both ordinary borrowing of individual lexical items and unavoidable interference (Coulmas, 2005).

Hereof, using code-switching does not confirm that one's linguistic competence is low due to alteration of codes; instead, the speaker is either a bilingual or multilingual speaker and is knowledgeable of the morphological, syntactical, lexical, and semantic features of codes. As stated by Estremera (2021), errors in pronunciation and morphology are at times risked. However, these errors do not hamper the communication cycle. Both the sender and the receiver of the message reach the common point of discourse. This idea is true; the most crucial aspect of communicating in any language variation is to convey the message clearly. Thus, the listener should exactly grasp what the speaker is purposively trying to say.

The most common example of code-switching in the Philippine context is Taglish (Tagalog and English). The country's L1 is Filipino, and L2 is English, making Filipinos bilingual speakers or even multilingual speakers, including some Spanish words and language varieties. Spain and America once colonized the Philippines.

Furthermore, one of the most popular taglish speakers is Kris Aquino, a famous celebrity and host. Some of her taglish lines are the following:

"Why are you buying twelve?"
Sabi ko, "Hello, I'm paying for it." Di ba?
(When Kris buys a whole bucket of chicken for herself)
Hello? Okay tapos I do have a salon in my new house.
(When Jhepoy Dizon says Kris is pulubi and taga- hugas)

These code-switching examples are intra- sentential code-switching since there are alterations of codes in every phrase. These taglish examples are quite comical, like when someone commits malapropism because of the lexis used and how the speaker delivers these lines sophisticatedly. But the semantic of these taglish lines are deep and wanted to imply something as revealed in Kris' statements. In addition, here are some of the popular hugot lines in Philippine cinema in Taglish delivered by respected actors in the country.

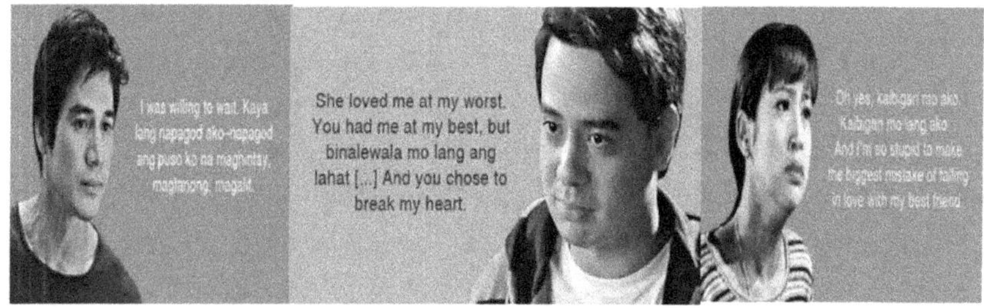

Herein, taglish in a script of a movie in the Philippines, especially if it's a love story, adds more intense emotion and feeling; it entices every Filipino fan to watch the film. Indeed, every viewer's attention is hooked due to heavy and strong hugot lines. On the contrary, malapropism is less popular than code-switching. In the writer's perspective of this paper, malapropism most of the time creates a barrier to the sender and receiver of the message due to its unique use of words. The semantics of the lexis is not literal but rather figurative. This needs a thorough understanding of pragmatics. This makes malapropism complicated to comprehend.

In most cases, malapropism usually does exist in American literary works. One of the most famous English writers is a fan of malapropism. William Shakespeare is known for his play on words, puns, and dialogic jargon. Several malapropisms are absurd and humorous, providing comedic relief and presenting insights into character natures (https://www.gradesaver.com).

The following excerpt is taken from Shakespeare's play used malapropism:

"If you be he, sir, I desire

*Some **confidence** with you" (II. iv. 64).*

Here, the Nurse wants to be a "confidant," a trusted friend to discuss private matters. The malapropism is confidence for confidant. In addition, it has been noted that the malapropism could be confidence for the conference. Regardless, confidence is still the wrong word choice (https://www.gradesaver.com).

*"She will **indite** him to some supper" (II. iv. 65).*

In this line spoken by Benvolio, the young man misuses "indite" for "invite." Indite is the writing of a sonnet or composition, suggesting Shakespeare is not only poking fun at the Nurse's request but poking fun at his craft (https://www.gradesaver.com).

"But I'll warrant you when I say so, she looks as pale as any clout in

*the **versal** world" (II. iv. 101- 102).*

Here, the nurse mistakenly uses "versal" for "universal," which is not only a humorous error but is a pun on the "versal world," meaning the world of playwriting (https://www.gradesaver.com).

Thus, these lines in the Romeo and Juliet play of William Shakespeare are rich in malapropism. A reader who'll read such work should carefully examine whether a particular word is used literally or figuratively. This requires analytical skill and wider background about the author's point of view as to why the writer intentionally used such malapropism in his work.

3. CONCLUSION

The research study used in this review paper thoroughly discussed the different features of code-switching and malapropism; delivered a broader and deep discussion on the said topics. Indeed, it provides essential ideas for the author of this paper in gathering opinions and facts for the said subjects. This reflection paper presents authentic and substantial material that will support the author's idea that whatever codes are used in discourse is not the basis of someone's intellect. This is supported by the idea that intelligence is defined as general cognitive problem-solving skills.

Mental ability is involved in reasoning, perceiving relationships and analogies, calculating, learning quickly, etc., and English is a language and a medium of communication (brainmatrix.com). If English is a language and a medium of communication, there's a need for people living in English-speaking countries to be fluent or at least be familiar with the code to live. But if a group of people lives in a non-

English- speaking country, there's probably no need to study and master English. Thus, it doesn't mean people who can't talk straight English has a lower IQ than those who can since English is simply one of the mediums to communicate; it's just all about a matter of surviving.

Further, the paper provides an example of code-switching in the Philippines, Taglish (Tagalog- English). And one of the country's most talked-about celebrities, Kris Aquino, a TV host, and actress, is fond of using Taglish whenever she speaks with a friend and other showbiz personalities. Every time Kris delivers her statements in Taglish, people are all ears because she perfectly manages the use of both codes; her command in switching L1 and L2 and vice versa is laudable. In addition, even students in Ateneo, DLSU, and other prestigious universities do have students who speak in Taglish, which makes them sound 'sosyal';. At the same time, listeners who don't know the speaker personally may infer that such interlocutor is 'maarte.'

Likewise, the paper also cited the most famous English playwright and poet, William Shakespeare, who even intentionally applied malapropism in Romeo and Juliet. Suppose a reader doesn't have an idea about malapropism. In that case, every semantic lexis will be taken literally because a specific word is used differently in a work of fiction from its original function.

In conclusion, even though code-switching and malapropism deviate from the standard norm of using any target language, especially English, these two (2) contribute significantly to the Philippine cinema industry, entertainment, and literary works as to Western literature. It does change the conventional code use, but this makes one's language unique since language is dynamic and inevitably evolving.

REFERENCES

Estremera, M. L. (2021, May 19). Linguistics Purpose and Historical Implications of Malapropism and Code-switching in the Philippines. Indonesian Journal of EFL and Linguistics, 6 (1), 169-186. Retrieved May 30, 2021, from

https://indonesianefljournal.org/index.php/ijefll/article/view/35
3

Gonzalo, Liezel. Hugot lines from pinoy movies.pinterest.com.
Retrieved May 30, 2021, from
https://www.google.com/amp/s/www.pinterest.com/amp/liezel
gonzalo/hugot-linesfrom-pinoy-movies/

Malapropism. (2021, May 21). Literary Terms.
https://www.google.com/amp/s/literaryterms.net/malapropism/
amp/

McArthur, T. (ed.).2005. The concise Oxford Companion to the
English Language. Oxford et al.: Oxford University Press.

Niles, Chad (2005, January). Code-Switching in Sociocultural
Linguistics. ResearchGate. Retrieved May   30,   2021,
from
https://www.researchgate.net/publication/23941967_code_Swi
tching_in_Sociocultural_Linguistics

Romeo and Juliet: Malapropism. (2017, May 22). GradeSaver.
https://www.gradesaver.com/romeo-and-juliet/q-and-
a/malapropism-335789

Shay, O. (2015, December). To switch or Not to Switch: Code-
switching in a Multilingual Country. ResearchGate. Retrieved
May 30, 2021, from
https://www.researchgate.net/publication/286903379_To_Swit
ch_or_Not_to_Switch_C ode-
switching_in_a_Multilingual_Country

Shofner, K. (2017, May 25). Linguistic Code-Switching: What it is and
Why it Happens. United Language   Group. Retrieved
         May   30,   2021,   from
https://www.globe.com/am/s/www.unitedlanguagegroup.com/
blog/linguistic-codeswitching%3fhs_amp=true

Weston, Daniel (2015, August 13). Mind the gap: What code-
switching in literature can teach us about code-switching.
Language and Literature: International Journal of Stylistics.
Retrieved   May   30,   2021,   from
https://journals.sagepub.com/doi/abs/10.1177/0963947015585
066

4

Multilingualism in the Philippines: Its Historical Implications to Code-Switching and Malapropism in Classroom Instruction

Synopsis: *Archeologically, the Philippines has been under the colonial rule of the Spanish, Americans, and the Japanese, which influenced Philippine culture, having diverse customs, traditions, and languages. According to Parekh's (2000) perspective, the Philippines is multicultural due to many cultures and the largely peaceful coexistence. Consequently, it can also be deemed that the Philippines is a multilingual country, attributing the diversity of its languages to the cultures of its people. This is supported by Mahadi & Jafari (2012), who, in their study, accentuated that language and culture are interrelated and that one has influence over the other— a reciprocal relationship between them both. Multilingualism in the Philippines has been one of the evident influences brought by colonialism. Having diverse dialects coupled with foreign languages being adapted and employed in communication does stem in influencing and alternating the language used to attain the chief purpose of communication. As an inappropriate word used inadvertently in place of another word, Malapropism became the unintentional escape of most speakers to have continuity in speech. Contrariwise, code-switching or language alternation functions as an effective medium of societal interactivity to link the gaps in linguistic incompetence between the mother tongue and the target language for clarification and communication purposes. Code-switching's main functions are equivalent comprehension, instructional procedures, cognition assurance, and socializing effects in a classroom setting. To* *realize the ultimate goal of utilizing code-switching in communication, teachers and educators play a significant role in employing the best strategies to explain the meaning of new words, check understanding, make students feel comfortable, and explain the grammatical differences between languages through the proper language alternation.*

1. INTRODUCTION

The Philippines is widely known as one of the countries that multilingualism is extensively embraced. The historical influence of colonialism that touches the culture of the Filipinos, most significantly its language and the indisputable fact of having 107 dialects, verifies that code-switching and malapropism veritably exist. Language alternation (CS) is a concrete phenomenon that transpires in the teaching and learning process as a second language speaker of English that bridges the communication gap in transferring and clarifying meanings to learners during classroom instruction. Significant claims were cited in the utilization of code-switching in education linked to its positive effects, specifically equivalent comprehension, instructional procedures, cognition assurance, and socializing.

2. DISCUSSION

Historically, the Philippines has been under Spanish, American, and Japanese colonial rule, which influenced Philippine culture, with diverse customs, traditions, and languages. Based on Parekh's (2000) perspective, the Philippines is multicultural due to the presence of many cultures and the generally peaceful coexistence of these cultures in society. Thus, it can also be said that the Philippines is a multilingual country, attributing the diversity of its languages to the cultures of its people. This is supported by Mahadi & Jafari (2012), who, in their study, pointed out that language and culture are interconnected, and that one has influence over the other— a reciprocal relationship between them both. With the existence of over a hundred dialects, Tagalog (now FILIPINO) became the national language of the Philippines as it is supported by the constitutional mandate of the Philippine government (Art. XIV, Sec. 6 1986 Constitution) based on existing Philippine languages as well as other foreign languages, with the hopes of uniting the nation through a common language, thus becoming the national language (Rubrico, 1997).

To supplement, Lewis et al. (2012) describe Tagalog as a widespread language with 45,000,000 L2 users. According to the report, it is not used in all official domains as English, the country's official language is more commonly used. L2 English users rank second, amounting to around 50% of the Philippine population (40,000,000 users) (Lewis et al., 2014). Being a multilingual country seems to influence and alter the dialects and other languages, resulting in malapropism and code-switching for better communication.

Malapropism is defined as an inappropriate word used inadvertently in place of another word with a related sound. For instance, the statement, "His capacity for hard liquor is *incredulous* (incredible)." It can be comical because they give rise to irrational speeches. Malapropism is also linked with the "slip of a tongue" word/phrases. Psycholinguistic or linguistic explanations can be viewed from the way language is produced. Speakers have plans (planning, linguistic, grammatical, phonological, and semantic units) for uttering. They have a vivid idea, but the articulatory mechanism does not cooperate with the cognitive mechanism (plan). When this happens, a slip occurs. The idea is right, but the expression comes out wrong while speakers are unaware of their errors. The idea may be right in the language of the mind, even though it is inadvertently wrong, as cited by Sternberg (1998:305).

Correspondingly, code-switching or language alternation potentially transpires when a speaker substitutes between two or more languages, or language variations, in the context of a single conversation. It functions as an effective medium of societal interactivity to link the linguistic incompetence gaps between the mother tongue and the target language for clarification and communication purposes. Switching between two languages in foreign language settings is a beneficial communicative strategy for bilingual students (Pollard, 2002). Educators conceive CS as a supporting communication tool for transferring and clarifying meanings to students during classroom instruction to avoid misunderstanding problems. Jingxia (2010) code-switching study pointed out that the term "code" denotes any system of signals, including numbers and words with real meanings. Furthermore, code was defined as a strategy used by more than one bilingual speaker for communication (Wardhaugh and Fuller, 2014).

According to Jdetawy (2011) and Alkhresheh (2015), some reasons for code-switching include interpreting the interlocutors' intentions and characterizing the morphosyntactical constraints by focusing on the location of the switches in the sentence. Hussein (1999) studied the psychological and social reasons that lead bilinguals to switch codes. Still, one principal reason for the learning process is that the students are not English proficient, and the linguistic range is not that wide. Hence, lecturers resort to code-switching to help their students understand materials and instruction better. In the Philippines, it has been an issue for debate whether or not to code-switch in teaching. Still, most individuals neglect the main goal of education, which is to impart learnings and knowledge to the learners, which became CS an integral part of the process.

The educator may start with the mother tongue (native language), then switch to either Filipino or English or vice versa depending on the matter being discussed. It is like teaching the kids to learn the alphabet. The process is enduring, but if proper strategy is employed, mastery will be achieved. It also goes the same way with the CS method. Learning won't exist if the material itself can't be understood. In this issue, teachers should know how to properly employ code-switching without disregarding the target language or the mode of instruction being utilized. This technique will also encourage the students to share their opinion without hesitations and doubt that they are probably committing errors in sentence construction and, at the same time, unconsciously adapting the code-switching strategy, which will serve as their avenue in using English more often. However, the attempts to transcode the native language to English encounter mispronounced or even misrepresented words. In one case of a five-year-old boy trying to answer his mother's question in English: "Francis, why don't you play the piano for your godmother?" And the boy's answer: "Mommy, I don't want. It's so *hirap eh*."[Because it's so difficult.]" You can observe how a boy at a young age used code-switching in expressing his feeling.

In this case, since Filipinos are multilingual and have "Tagalog(Filipino) as the national language and English as a secondary one, the meaning and the message could still be clearly understood in the communication process. Furthermore, various reasons were also cited why people, particularly teachers, do code-switching. Eldin (2014) indicated that speakers might switch codes to unify with the community, distinguish oneself, participate in public meetings, discuss a specific topic, express emotions, and persuade interlocutors.

In a classroom setting, utilizing the native language in learning and teaching serves three functions: the construction of engaging learners in interactions, establishing inter-subjectivity, and maintaining privacy. (Momenian & Samar, 2011). The functions of code-switching in English as Foreign Language (EFL) classrooms are investigated (Lee, 2010). He concluded that using a native language creates an opportunity for knowledge improvement, confidence promotion, and cultural and social identity development.

Additionally, educators' CS is relatively related to students' effective support and educational success (Badrul & Kamaruzaman, 2009). Similarly, code-switching is claimed to facilitate the EFL teaching and learning processes by finding out the hidden messages behind codeswitching (Tien & Liu, 2006). Equivalent comprehension, instructional procedures, cognition assurance, and socializing effects are the main functions of code-switching.

Bilgin and Rahimi (2013) and Sert (2005) revealed that code-switching is unconsciously applied in most language learning environments by teachers to serve some beneficial basic functions listed as topic switching, effective, and repetitive functions. In topic switch cases, teachers switch between languages based on the discussion topic. This can be mostly observed in grammar instruction since bilingual teachers use the native language while providing syntactic rules of the target language about dealing with particular grammatical points. Consequently, the student's attention will be directed to the new knowledge to facilitate comprehension, build solidarity and ensure a relaxing learning environment.

Another explanation for the functionality of code-switching in English Language Teaching settings is its effective expression of emotions. In this respect, bilingual teachers use code-switching to build intimate relations with students and create a supportive language environment. In addition to the topic switching and affective functions, the phenomenon also carries a repetitive function. In this sense, educators utilize code-switching to convey the necessary knowledge to clarify meaning and ensure efficient comprehension.

This comes in conformity with Rahimi and Jafari's (2011), who indicated that code-switching had been intensively applied while conducting vocabulary and grammar activities that encompass using equivalent words and expressions as well as replying in the native language to solve misunderstanding issues and to ensure complete and correct comprehension of the grammatical rules. Moreover, Badrul and Kamaruzaman (2009) and Lee (2010) revealed that teachers most often switch codes to explain the meaning of new words, check to understand, make students feel comfortable, and explain the grammatical differences between languages.

3. CONCLUSION

Multilingualism in the Philippines has been one of the evident influences brought by colonialism. Having diverse dialects coupled with foreign languages being adapted and employed in communication does stem in influencing and alternating the language used to attain the chief purpose of communication. As an inappropriate word used inadvertently in place of another word, Malapropism became the unintentional escape of most speakers to have continuity in speech.

Conversely, code-switching or language alternation functions as an effective medium of societal interactivity to link the gaps in linguistic incompetence between the mother tongue and the target language for clarification and communication purposes. Code-switching's main functions are equivalent comprehension, instructional procedures, cognition assurance, and socializing effects in a classroom setting.

To realize the ultimate goal of utilizing code-switching in communication, teachers and educators play a significant role in employing the best strategies to explain the meaning of new words, check understanding, make students feel comfortable, and explain the grammatical differences between languages through the proper language alternation.

REFERENCES

Alkhresheh, M. M. A. (2015). Code-switching and mixing of English and Arabic amongst Arab students at Aligarh Muslim University in India. International Journal of Scientific and Research Publications. Vol 5 (2), pp. 1-4.

Badrul Hisham Ahmad & Kamaruzaman Jussoff (2009). Teacher's code-switching in classroom instructions for low English proficient learners. English Language Teaching, 2(2), 49-55.

Bilgin, G. P., & Rahimi, A. (2013). EFL Teachers' Attitude toward Code-Switching: A Turkish Setting. International Journal of Linguistics, 5(5), pp-1.

Eldin, A. A. T. S. (2014). Socio-Linguistic Study of Code-Switching of the Arabic Language Speakers on Social Networking. International Journal of English Linguistics, 4(6), p78.

Estremera, M. L. (2021, May 19). Linguistics Purpose and Historical Implications of Malapropism and Code-switching in the Philippines. Indonesian Journal of EFL and Linguistics, 6 (1), 169-186. Retrieved May 30, 2021, from https://indonesianefljournal.org/index.php/ijefll/article/view/3 53

Hussein, R. F. (1999). Code-Alteration among Arab College Students. World Englishes, 18(2), 281-289

Jdetawy, L. F. A. (2011). Arabic-English Code-Switching among Arab Students at UUM, Malaysia. Language in India, 11(5).

Jingxia, Liu (2010). Teachers' Code-Switching to the L1 in EFL Classroom. The Open Applied Linguistics Journal 3(1). DOI:10.2174/1874913501003010010.

Lee, J.J. (2010). The Uniqueness of EFL Teachers: Perceptions of Japanese Learners. TESOL Journal, 1,1:23-48.

Lewis, G., Jones, B., & Baker, C. (2012a). Translanguaging: Origins and development from school to street and beyond. Educational Research and Evaluation, 18(7), 641-654.

Literary Devices: Definition of Examples and Terms. https://literarydevices.net/malapropism/.

Mahadi, T. S. T., & Jafari, S. M. (2012). Motivation, its types, and its impacts in language learning. International Journal of Business and Social Science, 3(24), 230–235.

Momenian, M. & Samar R. G. (2011). Functions of code-switching among Iranian advanced and elementary teachers and students. Educational Research and Reviews Vol. 6(13), pp. 769-777, 5. Available online at http://www.academicjournals.org/ERR ISSN 1990-3839 ©2011 Academic Journals.

Noor Al- Qaysi (2010) Review of Code-switching: Learners' and Educators' Perspectives, Malapropism as a slip of the tongue S Naiyf Al-Adab Journal, 142-151 https://www.researchgate.net/publication/328602468_Malapro pism_as_a_slip_of_the_tongue_S_Naiyf_Al-Adab_Journal_142-151.

Parekh, Bhikhu (2000). Rethinking Multiculturalism. Harvard University Press.

Pollard, Susan (2002). "The Benefit of Code-Switching within a Bilingual Education Program" Honors Projects. 2. https://digitalcommons.iwu.edu/hispstu_honproj/2.

Rahimi, A., & Jafari, Z. (2011). Iranian students' attitudes towards the facilitative and debilitative role of code-switching; types and moments of code-switching at EFL classroom. The Buckingham Journal of Language and Linguistics, 4, 15-28.

Rubrico, Jessie Grace U. (1997). "An Annotated Bibliography of Works and Studies on the History, Structure, and Lexicon of the Cebuano Language: 1610 to1996." Thesis (MA Linguistics), University of the Philippines, Diliman, Quezon City.

San Juan, E. Jr. (1999).The Paradox of Multiculturalism: Ethnicity and Identity in the Philippines https://www.univie.ac.at/Voelkerkunde/apsis/aufi/ethno/parad ox.htm.

Sert, O. (2005). The Functions of Code-Switching in ELT Classrooms. Online Submission, 11(8).

Sternberg, Robert, J. (1998). In Search of the Human Mind.2nd ed. USA: Harcourt Brace Company.

Wardhaugh, R., & Fuller, J. M. (2014). An introduction to sociolinguistics. John Wiley & Sons.

Wilkinson Daniel Wong Gonzales [Philippine Journal of Linguistics 47 (2016) 106 – 128] Trilingual Code-switching Using Quantitative Lenses: An Exploratory Study on Hokaglish. https://files.eric.ed.gov/fulltext/ED571766.pdf.

5

Malapropism and Code-Switching: Significant Tools for Classroom Instruction

Synopsis: *Considering linguistic phenomena, these call for the need to consider malapropism and code-switching significant in classroom instruction. Malapropism is roughly defined as a statement in which some target expressions are substituted by different lexis that is usually similar in articulation. However, code-switching shifts from one linguistic code (a language or dialect) to another, depending on the social milieu or everyday situation. As a language teacher, the ultimate goal of our lessons is for our students to speak, understand and communicate in English. We can encourage this in the classroom by creating an open and engaging atmosphere, so our students feel comfortable enough to talk to their classmates. This presupposes getting to know each other, having a chat, and collaborating to accomplish their language goals.*

Conversely, communication breakdowns may occur during the learning process and can cause difficulty among students in learning the language. According to Jenkins (2000), the biggest cause of communication breakdowns is mispronounced or misunderstood phonemes that are common to non-native speakers of English. To supplement, a limited cache of vocabulary words directly contributes to language blockades. To conclude, the existence of malapropism and code-switching in the Philippines can be construed as having a positive and negative impact on learners. It may ostensibly be concluded that the impression of code-switching as a barrier to learning seems to be the predominant view amongst learners and teachers. Any positive effects of code-switching are not yet widely acknowledged.

1. INTRODUCTION

This paper calls for the need to consider malapropism and code-switching significant in classroom instruction considering the linguistic phenomena. Malapropism is roughly defined as an utterance where some target expression is replaced by a different expression that is similar in pronunciation. In comparison, code-switching is a process of shifting from one linguistic code (a language or dialect) to another, depending on the social context or conversational setting. In applied linguistics, these two types of linguistic phenomena can be categorized as performance errors in which learners make errors when they are tired or hurried.

Normally, this type of error is not serious and can be overcome with little effort by the learner. In a classroom where the English language is considered a second language, English teachers employ code-switching to minimize students' miscomprehension or difficulties in understanding the English lesson. Likewise, malapropism is also inevitable among learners in classroom instruction. Language learners frequently commit malapropism when they have something to say but forget the right term; instead, they utter the word similar in pronunciation.

2. DISCUSSION

As a language teacher, the ultimate goal of our lessons is for our students to speak, understand and communicate in English. We can encourage this in the classroom by creating an open and engaging atmosphere, so our students feel comfortable enough to talk to their classmates. This means getting to know each other, having a chat, and cooperating and collaborating to achieve their language goals. However, communication breakdowns may occur during the learning process and cause difficulty among students in learning the language. According to Jenkins (2000), the biggest cause of communication breakdowns is mispronounced or misunderstood phonemes that are common to non-native speakers of English.

In addition, limited vocabulary also contributes to language barriers. These can be frustrating, but as language teachers, we must learn to cope with these challenges encountered by the learners.

In the article presented, malapropism and code-switching can aid in learning the second language when such drawbacks to communication are converted into rich opportunities for meaningful classroom tête-à-tête. As per experience, it is possible since our goal is to successfully deliver the lesson to various types of learners in a classroom. According to (Bista 2010:1), an important teaching skill is transferring knowledge to students clearly and efficiently. So code-switching can be a useful tool in the classroom for both teachers and students. The teacher uses code-switching to share the necessary knowledge for the students for clarity (Wei, 2000).

Therefore, following the instruction in the target language, the teacher code switches to the native language to clarify meaning. In this way, it stresses the importance of foreign language content for efficient comprehension. However, the tendency to repeat the instruction in the native language may lead to some undesired student behavior. A learner who is sure that a native language translation will follow the instruction in a foreign language may lose interest in listening to the former instruction, which will have negative academic consequences. The student is exposed to foreign language discourse limitedly. The teacher's use of code-switching is not always performed consciously, which means that the teacher is not always aware of the functions and outcomes of the code-switching process. "The use of code-switching, therefore, is a conscious choice, especially because speakers are aware of the social consequences of this particular action" (Metila, 2009, p.46).

Therefore, in some cases, it may be regarded as an automatic and unconscious behavior. Various studies have shown that code-switching benefits students and teachers. These studies also maintain that classroom code-switching should be allowed, and this is due to the supposed advantages that code-switching gives to learning. According to Metila (2009, p.44), "the pedagogical and communicative functions of classroom code-switching justify its use in teaching and learning contexts, but it is recommended that code-switching be restricted to informal classroom activities."

Estremera (2021) stated that colonization is a historical basis for malapropisms and code-switching in the Philippines. This claim was supported by sample dialogues presented in the article wherein the two linguistic phenomena are used. Malapropism and code-switching are part of Filipino culture and eventually become chronic language trends. Hence, these linguistic phenomena are acceptable as long as it does not hinder the communication between speakers.

Likewise, code-switching can be more functional in a classroom setting for explaining concepts, emphasizing, checking for understanding, developing vocabulary, etc. In this case, some restrictions on the use of code-switching must be established by teachers in the classroom, and learners should code-switch only when there is an urgent case.

3. CONCLUSION

The existence of malapropism and code-switching in the Philippines can be perceived as positively and negatively impacting learners. It may be concluded that the impression of code-switching as a barrier to learning seems to be the prevalent view amongst both learners and teachers. Any positive effects of code-switching are not yet widely recognized. But undeniably, code-switching is a common language practice of English teachers during classroom instructions and uses it as an instructional strategy for several academic purposes.

Furthermore, code-switching is adapted by a teacher not only as a communicative device (Adendorf, 1996; Myers-Scotton, 1995) and an instrument to enhance discourse such as emphasizing a point (Gal, 1979) and mitigating a message (Koziol, 2000), but also, most importantly, as a scaffolding device that effectively facilitates and optimizes students' learning in culturally and linguistically diverse classrooms (Lin, 2008). Therefore, this linguistic phenomenon is acceptable only that teachers at the school must establish some restrictions on the use of code-switching, and learners should code-switch only when there is an urgent case.

REFERENCES

Adendorff, R. (1996). The functions of code-switching amongst high school teachers and students in Kwazulu and implications for teacher education. In K. M. Bailey and D. Nunan (eds) Voices from the Language Classroom: Qualitative Research in Second Language Education (pp. 388-406). New York: Cambridge University Press.

Bista, K., (2010.) 'Factors of Code-Switching among Bilingual English Students In the University Classroom: A Survey. English for Specific Purposes World, Volume 9, pp.1-19.

Estremera, M. L. (2021). Linguistic purpose and historical implications of malapropism and code-switching in the Philippines. Indonesian Journal of EFL and Linguistics, 6(1), 169. https://doi.org/10.21462/ijefl.v6i1.353

Gal, S. (1979). Language shift: Social determinants of linguistic change in bilingual Austria. New York: Academic Press.

Jenkins, J. (May 2000). The Phonology of English as an International Language. Oxford University Press. https://www.researchgate.net/publication/244511317_The_Pho nology_of_English_as_an_International_Language.

Koziol, J. M. (2000). Code-switching between Spanish and English in contemporary American society. Unpublished MA thesis, St. Mary's College of Maryland.

Lin, A. (2008). Code-switching in the classroom: Research paradigms and approaches. In: Hornberger, Nancy ed. Encyclopedia of Language and Education. New York: Springer, p.3464–3477.

Metila, R. A. (2009). Decoding the Switch: The Functions of Code-switching in the Classroom. Education quarterly. 67 (1), 44-61

Myers-Scotton, C. (1995). Social motivations for code-switching: Evidence from Africa. Oxford: Clarendon Press.

Rodrigo (December 21, 2016). Code-switching: The Effects for Students and Teachers. The Write Pass Journal. https://writepass.com/journal/2016/12/code-switching-the-effects- for-students-and-teachers/.

Thompson, Roger M. (2003) Filipino English and Taglish - Language switching from multiple perspectives. Philadelphia: John Benjamin Publishing Company.

Touchie, H. (1986). Second Language Learning Errors Their Types, Causes, and Treatment. JALT   Journal, Volume 8, No. I, p.76. https://jalt-publications.org/sites/default/files/pdf-article/art5_8.pdf.

Wei, L. (2000). The Bilingualism Reader. London: Routledge

6

Malapropism and Code Switching: A Lifelong Bridge to Language Barrier of the Students in the Classroom using Social Media Platform

Synopsis: *The multifaceted issue of language evolution continues to puzzle because of its links with culture, social behavior, and the human mind's development. Language, besides technology, is the high point of human evolutionary achievement. As Schumann(1986) points out, acculturation can be a social mechanism that catalyzes new identities and language change. When people are speaking the same language, they do not necessarily share the same identity. Hence, language acts as a mediator of personal and social identity, and when one language is used, multiple identities and second languages may provide a background lexicon. Identity is created from language to adapt to different situations. With this growing trend in linguistic globalization, bilingualism has become very common. To meet the communication demands, teachers, students and speakers frequently switch from one language to another for meaningful discourse. Lifelong learning can enhance our understanding of the world around us, provide us with more and better opportunities and improve our quality of life. The primary goal of education and development of the curriculum is for quality education and to produce globally competitive graduates and lifelong learning and skills. This opened its horizon for learning a second language, thus incorporating English specifically in the curriculum, not just a second language. Rather, it is also used as a medium of instruction. With this event, hence the rise of bilingualism and bilingual education is evident. Teachers play an important role and a great influence in the language learning of the students. In the classroom, code-switching is inevitable, wherein teachers become an equilibrium in the communicative* *process. Code-switching and malapropism are essential tools for attaining objectives in content-based instruction and making communication more effective and meaningful.*

1. INTRODUCTION

Nelson Mandela once said that "If you talk to a man in a language he understands, that goes to his head. If you talk to him in his language, that goes to his heart". When you make an effort to speak someone else's language, even if it's just basic phrases here and there, you are saying to them, 'I understand that you have a culture and identity that exists beyond me. I see you as a human being" Nevertheless, learning a language gives not only communication skills but also a way of understanding different perspectives and how different cultures see the world through good communication.

Nowadays, a seismic and quicksilver change happens in technology as well as language. We've noticed that language changes across space, social groups and varies across time. Generation by generation, pronunciations evolve, new words are borrowed or invented, the meaning of old words drifts, and morphology develops or decays. The complex issue of language evolution continues to perplex because of its associations with culture, social behavior, and the human mind's development. Language, besides technology, is the pinnacle of human evolutionary achievement.

Schumann (1986) states that acculturation can be a social mechanism that catalyzes new identities and language change. When people are speaking the same language, they do not necessarily share the same identity. Hence, language acts as a mediator of personal and social identity, and when one language is used, multiple identities and second languages may provide a background lexicon. Identity is created from language to adapt to different situations. This growing trend in linguistic globalization, bilingualism has become very common. To meet the communication demands, teachers, students and speakers frequently switch from one language to another for meaningful discourse. The alternation between languages is known as code-switching coupled with a malapropism, which is the mistaken use of an incorrect word in place of a word with related sounds that inevitably occur in every classroom interaction and society. According to Fantini (1985), Genishi (1981); and, Huerta (1980), they argue that Code Switching should not be seen as a handicap but rather as an opportunity for children's language development.

Consequently, teachers resulting to code-switching for further clarification of instruction and the extent of complete communication. In many instances when learners fail to communicate through the medium of instruction, Code Switching has been demonstrated to be an effective teaching and learning technique in schools that use a second language as a medium of instruction (Aichum, 2003; Brock-Utne, 2002; Huerta-Macias & Quintero, 1992; Ogechi, 2002; Zabrodskaja, 2007).

Additionally, code-switching and malapropism are considered extremely important aspects of cognitive development and social communication for students in an inevitable forthcoming. Technology is one way of fast communication; it is essential that social media integration in classroom and community using code-switching and malapropism language.

Moreover, Hung and Yeun (2010) said that social media networking technologies are used in various contexts for improving communication affectivity. They added that learning is a social activity that specifically benefits from social networking usage. It provides opportunities for learning inside and outside the classrooms and increases the interaction among learners. The occurrences of malapropism and code-switching discourse make a difference; therefore, utilizing these linguistic spectacles of the students using social media platforms in the classroom and society can build good rapport in discourse, acquire lifelong learning, and bridge the gap of a language barrier in a comprehensive communication that occurred in a productive interaction.

2. DISCUSSION

Code-switching and Malapropism are phenomena that exist in bilingual societies where people have the opportunity to use two or more languages to communicate. According to Trousdale (2010), code-switching is the linguistic situation where a speaker alternates between two varieties (code) in conversation with others who have a similar linguistic repertoire. Code-switching can also occur when transitioning from verbal to non-verbal communication." Bilinguals can speak more than one language and code-switch and use their languages as resources to find better ways to convey meaning. Mostly, code-switching and malapropism occur in English classrooms in upper secondary school every day.

Furthermore, Bernardo (2005) said that code-switching can be a legitimate and potent resource for learning and teaching for bilingual students and teachers and that we [Filipinos in general and stakeholders in Philippine education in particular] should relax our language prescription in formal school environments to allow students and teachers to benefit from the use of this productive resource of developing knowledge and understanding. Under the name of malapropisms, Fay and Cutler (1997) have examined a variety of speech errors. However, malapropisms in the classical sense are not speech errors: they are what the speaker intended to say and would be willing to repeat.

Although Malapropism is inherently ridiculous or funny and heavily based on laughable and even off-color, it's been effective in semantics. In school, where teachers are held accountable for imparting knowledge and delivering instruction to lifelong learning, these two linguistic phenomena are mostly used. Code-switching has often been used as a means of clarification or explanation, especially by those who are not bilingual. For some whys and wherefores, aside from descriptive or to keep one of the speakers from understanding them, also, it builds good rapport in discourse.

In the study of Sert (2005), code-switching in the ELT classroom finds that code-switching is used either in the teachers' or the students' discourses.   The results show that students who cannot express themselves clearly in one language often switch languages to avoid difficulties. Thus, affective functions are important in expressing emotions and building a relationship between the teacher and the student. Linsin (2012) assumed that rapport is more than a connection you make with your students based on their positive feelings for you. When they like and trust you, and when you in turn like and believe in them, you'll form a bond that makes classroom management a lot easier.

In like manner, when you establish rapport in the classroom, the flow of the teaching-learning process creates an understanding in instructions and in conveying information to the students, resulting in lifelong learning to the language barrier. The teacher alters his or her language according to the topic being taught in issue switching to clarify the meaning of a word and stresses importance on the foreign language content for better comprehension. Once the students develop the ability to recognize the differences between their home dialect and formal English, they can then practice code-switching using the appropriate language in the proper context at the proper time.

Language is pivotal in our inter-related society with rich linguistic typologies that need comprehension to proper communication. When a student's accustomed to malapropism and codeswitching, they can adapt and adjust easily in this changing world and be a globally competitive citizen. Considering that language evolves, malapropism and codeswitching occurrences on social media which has been influential to learners.

A case study about the usage of code-switching in social media in Oman by Noor Al-Qaysi, Mostafa Al Emran (2017) noticed that 86.40 % of the student's code switches on social networks, whereas 81 % of the educators do so. Furthermore, results indicated that students are highly positive in their attitudes toward code-switching in social media. Therefore, social media code-switching has been beneficial to the students for future preferences and the educators. Social media websites make it easy to communicate with colleagues anytime, anywhere (Salloum et al., 2017). Social networking websites provide a reliable platform for higher educational institutions. Similarly, Schlenkrich and Sewry (2012) have likewise underpinned that social media sites help users make relationships and broadcast information among social networks. The majority of educators, students, parents, and businesses utilize tools in social media for communication with each other in a quick, effective method.

Tess (2013) said that social media are increasingly apparent within higher educational contexts. Instructors use social media technology as an educational tool to improve teaching and support active learning for learners. Through codeswitching and malapropism languages, students acquire lifelong learning and integrate social media into their current method that can be useful for comprehensive communication.

According to a study revealed by Rimmer (2007), social media is defined as data collection, representation, processing, and dissemination of race, religion, books, movies, and relationship status shared between friends, family members, and strangers. In this sense, Mazer et al. (2007), social networking sites allow both educators and students to develop a mutual relationship; and create a positive learning experience for both parties. The widespread use of malapropism and code-switching in schools consider social media an important part of learning. Students used Google Plus, YouTube, Google Docs, and Facebook as educational tools used as an online community that can assist their learning. Based on the survey results of Bermudez et al. (2016), social media provides a fruitful source for their learning, and they enjoy learning while using them.

According to a study conducted by Akbari et al. (2016), as per Astin's Theory of Student engagement, the most significant issue in teaching and learning is increased students' engagement in education. Thus, the study analyzed the impact of network usage on students' engagement, learning, and motivation. Furthermore, an increasing number of research papers address the role of code-switching and malapropism in education for the students' lifelong learning that serves as a bridge to a language barrier. Social media has played a significant role in promoting English language learning processes. A wide range of language proficiency makes code-switching a necessary tool in overcoming language barriers. Communication becomes difficult in situations where people don't understand each other's language. This is the most common communication barrier which causes misunderstandings and misinterpretation between people. Code-switching and malapropism have frequently acted as a tool to cut across the language barrier and aid in understanding.

According to Damra & Qudah (2012), teachers believe that the use of the native language can explain grammar rules. They consider that teachers who know the students' native language have more advantages than those who do not. This supports Akinson's (2012) idea, which contends that the mother tongue's potential in any attempts to develop. The findings in the study of Wilkerson (1985) indicated that the instructors use code-switching to save time, avoid ambiguity, and establish authority.

Indeed, teachers find means to deliver the lessons to the student's understanding and a helpful tool in understanding the lesson. Teachers often practice code-switching in the classroom for a certain reason to make the students understand the instruction and to have an effective, productive interaction and active participation. Today, amid a pandemic, teachers, administrators, leaders, and organizations have made a way to make the students' learning effective. The delivery of instructions came up with blended learning where online learning through radio-based instructions, television, and other useful mode or avenue to transfer learning existed.

Code-switching is used to reach, educate, inform, deliver messages, and increase the students' level of awareness with sight, sound, and motion of what is happening worldwide. Billones (2012) examined identifiable patterns of code-switched lexical items from Tagalog/Cebuano, two of the largest spoken languages in the Philippines, in English news articles from the Philippines' printed newspaper. He concluded that the presence of code-switching is not just confined to function as a "bilingual substitutional tool but as a creative process that reinforces a growing global language identity out of multiple language speakers in a world of shifting nationalities and boundaries. The influential code-switching aspect in social media, through television, goes behind and beyond expectations in society. Thompson (2003) analyzed 292 Philippine television commercials in 1997 and found that English was the prime language in TV commercials. He further noted that code-switching to English upheld good character and fortune and items such as cigarettes, drinks, and gambling events. The other study was performed by Gerlan (2008), who found that code-switched advertisements were predominant over those solely in English or in Filipino. He also posted three important points. First, code-switching is a strategy of advertisers to attain a high level of information retention through memorability. Second, in code-switching, two languages are involved: the first language of the speech community and English, the global language.

Last, code-switching is a strategy that creates social identities that the audience can relate to or discover. Therefore, to be able to communicate, language understanding is an important factor in reaching the audience. Moreover, Bernardo (2005) said that code-switching can be a legitimate and potent source for learning and teaching for bilingual students and teachers and that Filipinos in general and stakeholders in Philippine education should relax or languages prescription in formal school environments to allow students and teachers to benefit from the use of this productive resource of developing knowledge and understanding. Subsequently, the influence of social media through the language of code-switching and malapropism, whether used inside or outside the classroom, has been supported with empirical evidence for the students' lifelong learning to understand the text and start a good conversation.

3. CONCLUSION

Lifelong learning can enhance our understanding of the world around us, provide us with more and better opportunities and improve our quality of life. The primary goal of education and development of the curriculum is for quality education and to produce globally competitive graduates and lifelong learning and skills. This opened its horizon for learning a second language, thus incorporating English specifically in the curriculum, which is not just a second language rather, it is also used as a medium of instruction. With this event, hence the rise of bilingualism and bilingual education is evident. Teachers play an important role and a great influence in the language learning of the students.

In the classroom, code-switching is inevitable, wherein teachers become an equilibrium in the communicative process. Code-switching and malapropism are essential tools for attaining objectives in content-based instruction and making communication more effective and meaningful. According to Bennett and Dunne (2002), the language used during classroom instruction should not be emphasized. Still, a language should be used as an instrument of learning. Once the learner has developed a new understanding, he or she needs to reflect and exchange ideas and views with other learners and the teachers to consolidate this or her learning. Classroom talk, be it in the mother tongue, or the English language, or Code-Switching and Malapropism, indicates the teacher's state of the learners' understanding.

Code-switching and malapropism language integration through social media websites-built strategy and positive attitudes towards learners. Teachers and students are using various online tools to cater to different requirements. Social media and education go hand in hand in the modern world, which benefits learners and help fill in the learning gaps. Code-switching and malapropism used in social media provide vast information, generate ideas, and connect students to the world. Liao (2014) employed a reasonable integration of an old theory called Community Language Learning with new technology for future language classrooms. It investigated how the Community Language Learning method can be the most effective approach in a flipped EFL classroom using new technology with Facebook. Being able to communicate with someone effectively is a strong basis for forming friendships.

People's primary languages can be different, but that does not mean that communication cannot occur. Just by putting in the effort to find ways to communicate with someone shows willingness to learn the perspective of others. Although code-switching and malapropism were used for many reasons, the most useful bridge was built between the language barrier and the students' lifelong learning.

REFERENCES

Aichum, L. (2003). Teacher Code-Switching in EFL classroom. Retrieved May 5, 2006, from http://www.beionline.com/tutor/2003collection/liuachum.htm.

Al-Qaysi, Noor, Al-Emran, Mostafa (2017). Code-switching Usage in social media: A Case Study from Oman. International Journal of Information Technology and Language Studies. Retrieved from https://www.researchgate.net/publication/318982373_Codeswitching_Usage_in_Social_Media_A_Case_Study_from_Oman

Banatao, Mary Ann B.; Malenab-Temporal Conchita (2018). Code Switching in Television Advertisement. TESOL International Journal Vol. 13 Issue 4. ISSN 2094-3938. Retrieved from https://files.eric.ed.gov/fulltext/EJ1244132.pdf

Bermudez, C. M., Prasad, P. W. C., Alsadoon, A., & Hourany, L. (2016). Students perception on the use of social media to learn English within secondary education in developing countries. In 2016 IEEE Global Engineering Education Conference (EDUCON) (pp. 968-973). IEEE.

Bernardo, A. B. I. (2005). Bilingual code-switching as a resource for learning and teaching: Alternative reflections on the language and education issue in the Philippines. In D. T. Dayag & J. S. Quakenbush (Eds.), Linguistics and language education in the Philippines and beyond: A festschrift in honor of Ma. Lourdes S. Bautista (pp. 151-169). Manila, the Philippines: Linguistic Society of the Philippines.

Borlongan, Ariane Macalinga. Reflecting on the Use of Code-Switching in the Philippine Education Today. TESOL Journal Vol. 7, pp. 78-80@2012. Retrieved from https://tesol-internationaljournal.com/wp-content/uploads/2013/11/V7_A7.pdf

Brock-Utne, B. (2002). The most recent developments concerning the debate on language of instruction in Tanzania. Institute for Education Research. Oslo: University of Oslo

Estremera, M. L. (2021, May 19). Linguistics Purpose and Historical Implications of Malapropism and Code- switching in the Philippines. Indonesian Journal of EFL and Linguistics, 6 (1), 169-186.   Retrieved   May   30,   2021,   from https://indonesianefljournal.org/index.php/ijefll/article/view/35

Fantini, A. E. (1985). Language acquisition of a bilingual child: A sociolinguistic perspective (to age ten). Clevedon, U.K.: Multilingual Matters.

Fay, David and Anne Cutler (1977). "Malapropisms and the Structure of the Mental Lexicon," Linguistic Inquiol 8.3.505-20.

Genishi, C. (1981). Code-switching in Chicano six-year olds. In R. Duran (Ed.), Latino language and communicative behavior (pp. 133-152). Norwood, New Jersey: Ablex.

Huerta, A. G. (1980). The acquisition of bilingualism: A codeswitching approach. In R. Bauman, & J. Sherzer (Eds.), Language and Speech in American society: A compilation of research papers in sociolinguistics (pp. 1-28). Austin, Texas: Southwest Educational Development Lab.

Huerta-Macias, A., & Quintero, E. (1992). Code-Switching, bilingual and biliteracy: Case Study. Duluth: University of Minnesota.

Hung, T. H & Yuen, S. C. (2010). **Educational use of social networking technology in high education** Teaching in Higher Education, 15 (2010), pp. 703-714 CrossRefView Record in Scopus Google Scholar.

Khan, Aalia Mehar (2014). Social aspects of Code-Switching: An analysis of Pakistani Television Advertisements. Information Management and Business Review Vol 6, No.6 pp.269-279, December 2014 (ISSN 2220-3796) Retrieved from https://core.ac.uk/download/pdf/288022309.pdf

Linsin, M. (2011, May 7). Why you should never, ever be friends with your students. Retrieved May 4, 2018 from https://www.smartclassroommanagement.com/2011/05/07/nev erbe-friends-with-students/

Mazer, J.P., Murphy, R.E., and Simonds, C.J. (2007). I'll See You On "Facebook": The Effects of Computer-Mediated Teacher Self-Disclosure on Student Motivation, Affective Learning, and

Classroom Climate. Communication Education, vol. 56, no. 1, pp 1–17.

Moore, Daniele. Case Study Code Switching and Learning in the Classroom. International Journal of Bilingual Education and Bilingualism 5(5):279-293. Retrieved from https://www.researchgate.net/publication/261586361_Codeswi tching_and_Learning_in_the_Classroom

Ogechi, N. O. (2002). Trilingual Code Switching in Kenya-evidence from Ekegusii, Kiswahili, English and Sheng (Unpublished doctoral dissertation). Hamburg: Universitat Hamburg.

Rabe, Andrea (1997). Breaking language barrier through the use of code switching. Retrieved from http://ematusov.soe.udel.edu/final.paper.pub/_pwfsfp/000000b 1.htm

Rimmer, I. (2007) 'Social Networking', iWeek, no. 115, 13 September, pp 15–18

Salloum, S. A., Al-Emran, M., Monem, A. A., & Shaalan, K. (2017). A Survey of Text Mining in Social Media: Facebook and Twitter Perspectives. Advances in Science, Technology and Engineering Systems Journal.

Samhan, Alaa Hussein. Social Aspects in Social Media: Code Switching and Code Mixing in Twitter. Research on Humanities and Social Studies. ISSN 2224-5766 (Paper) ISSN 2225- 0484 (Online) Vol. 7, No. 18,2017. Retrieved form https://core.ac.uk/download/pdf/234676096.pdf

Schlenkrich, L., & Sewry, D. (2012). Factors for successful use of social networking sites in higher education. South African Computer Journal, 49.

Schumann, J. (1986). Research on the acculturation model for second language acquisition. Journal of Multilingual and Multicultural Development, 7, 379-392. https://doi.org/10.1080/01434632.1986.9994254.

Sert, O. (2005). The functions of code-switching in ELT classrooms. The Internet TESL Journal, XI (8).Retrieved June 23rd, 2012, from http://iteslj.org/Articles/Sert-CodeSwitching.html.

Sutricno, Bejo; Ariesta, Yessika (2019). Beyond the use of Code Mixing by Social Media Influencers in Instagram. Advances in Language and Literary Studies. ISSN:2203-4714. Retrieved from https://files.eric.ed.gov/fulltext/EJ1255244.pdf

Tess, P. A. (2013). The role of social media in higher education classes (real and virtual)–A literature review. Computers in Human Behavior, 29(5), A60-A68.

Trousdale, G. (2010). An introduction to English Sociolinguistics. Endingburgh University press.

Zabrodskaja, A. (2007). Russian-Estonian code-switching in the university. Arizona working papers in SLA & Teaching, 14, 123-139.

7

"Taglish": The Filipino Way of having a Discourse

Synopsis: This paper highlights the code-switching and malapropism phenomenon in the Philippines in the context of Tagalog + English "Taglish" in a discourse between two people. Filipinos speak several languages, such as dialects from different regions across the archipelago and the English language. Despite individual differences, all bilinguals share the ability to act in their native language, in their second language, and to switch back and forth between the two languages they know (Van Hell, 1998). Study shows that two-thirds of the Filipino population is fluent in English, making the Philippines the largest English-speaking country ranking 15th out of 80 countries in 2017. This paper also describes the bilingual culture of the Filipinos, especially with the linguistic structure of Tagalog-English practice. The paper will reveal why the language mentioned earlier is frequently used by Filipinos when communicating with others. The Tagalog-English (Taglish) code-switching phenomenon has traveled a long distance. It began with assigning small portions of Tagalog-English code-switching to one language and formulating rules for such mixing. And it has advanced to describe the uses of Taglish in Philippine society and its importance as a mode of discourse and a linguistic resource.

1. INTRODUCTION

The Philippines has a long history of different colonizers. For more than 300 years, Spaniards colonized the Philippines, which engraved its Christian views on religion and became the baseline for Filipino surnames. The Japanese were also included in the list, but the American occupation in the Philippines was the most remembered among others. They stayed in the country for around 40 years, and up to this day, the English language is prominent as it is widespread and taught in schools.

Filipinos speak several languages of their own, such as dialects from different regions across the archipelago and the English language. Despite individual differences, all bilinguals share the ability to act in their native language, in their second language, and to switch back and forth between the two languages they know (Van Hell, 1998). Study shows that two-thirds of the Filipino population is fluent in English, making the Philippines the largest English-speaking country ranking 15th out of 80 countries in 2017. Although numerous can speak in English, not as many can translate English words to Tagalog. Those who can alter Tagalog and English in informal discourse are a feature of the linguistic repertoire of educated, middle- and upper-class Filipinos.

Today, two official national languages are recognized in the Philippines: Filipino (a standardized version of Tagalog) and English. These are the languages taught in school, used in workplaces and law, etc. At least, that is how things appear. In practice, however, people have adapted both the languages into one we refer to as "Taglish."

2. DISCUSSION

Taglish is a mixture of two languages, the code-switching of English and Tagalog. It uses Tagalog words, phrases, clauses, and sentences in English discourse, or vice-versa. The term is also occasionally used generically to switch between a Philippine language (not necessarily Tagalog) and English.

Taglish goes beyond the borrowing of words or ready-made phrases; it involves switching between languages. It is the language of informality among middle-class, college-educated, urbanized Filipinos. It was initially looked down upon and viewed as a corruption of Tagalog or English, but it is now a lingua franca in Philippine cities.

Taglish has been described as "a very widespread predominantl y spoken "mixed" language variety, whose phonology, morphology, syntax, and semantics have been greatly influenced by English and

Tagalog (Tangco and Ricardo, 2002). Taglish is common throughout the Tagalog-speaking region of the Philippines and is largely considered "the normal, acceptable conversation style of speaking and writing" (Goulet 1971, 83).

Among educated *Tagalogs*, mixing is considered the normal, acceptable conversational style of speaking and writing. The bilingual use borrowings generously, shifts from one language to another easily, and does not resist the adoption of loans (Goulet, 1971). Ultimately, mixing both Tagalog and English provides the best of both worlds to get an idea across.

Admit it, we all are guilty of using Tagalog and English in sentences or more often in our usual conversation and dialogues with people. It may sound funny or irrational at times, but it has become an effective tool for people who have difficulty translating terms in one language. More than being a code-switch, *Taglish* also practices malapropism. Malapropism is an unfitting word used unintentionally in place of another word with a similar sound. Malapropisms can be funny sounding since they give rise to illogical statements such as "In all fairness ha, you we're exceptionally good." For others, they might not notice, but the message is irrational and redundant.

With the end goal of conveying your thoughts in the most convenient and way, language can have its meaning. Language can be just a single language for some, but for many other Filipinos, it can be a mixture of Tagalog and English, which they find more convenient to express their thoughts. As long as the ideas, perspectives, and opinions successfully come across the other person, discourse will always occur.

3. CONCLUSION

The Tagalog-English (*Taglish*) code-switching phenomenon has traveled a long distance. It began with assigning small portions of Tagalog-English code-switching to one language and formulating rules for such mixing. And it has advanced to describe the uses of Taglish in Philippine society and its importance as a mode of discourse and a linguistic resource.

It has branched out from simple communication between two people through casual conversations but eventually reaching the academe. The Komisyon sa Wikang Filipino even stressed out that we cannot completely translate into Filipino because translating means making the word sounds absurd; instead, they urge the use of "paghihiram" ng salita. Can you translate shampoo in Filipino? Maybe it is about time we normalize Taglish as the Filipino way of having a discourse.

References:

Estremera, M. L. (2021, May 19). Linguistics Purpose and Historical Implications of Malapropism and Code-switching in the Philippines. Indonesian Journal of EFL and Linguistics, 6 (1), 169-186. Retrieved May 30, 2021, from https://indonesianefljournal.org/index.php/ijefll/article/view/35 3

Gustilo, L. E., & Go, M. A. C. (2013). Tagalog or Taglish: The Lingua Franca of Filipino Urban Factory Workers. Philippine ESL Journal, 10, 1–87. https://www.academia.edu/15556421/Tagalog_or_Taglish_the _Lingua_Franca_of_Filipino_Urban_Factory_Workers.

Lesada, J. D. (2017). Taglish In Metro Manila: An Analysis Of Tagalog-English Code-Switching (thesis).

8

Linguistic Purpose and Historical Implications of Malapropism and Code Switching: A Communicative Competence

Synopsis: *This paper is an attempt to explore the term communicative competence in a foreign language. It goes through the various definitions and some models of communicative competence, especially those most common models of Hymes (1972), Canale and Swain (1980), and Alcon 2000. It shows how the term 'communicative competence' came into existence during the 1970s. It has become a major aim for teaching and learning English as a foreign or second language in many countries. The study cited evidence that Malapropism and code-switching were observed long before American colonization (Estremera, 2021). The ability of the Filipinos to adapt to foreign languages made them good speakers and good writers like Dr. Jose Rizal. In handling English subjects, teachers often have difficulties; reading, writing, and speaking skills. Students are not proficient in the English language, particularly in speaking language. Therefore, English teachers are forced to switch to make the students understand the subject matter. Switching from one language to another language is an effective way to establish classroom communication continuously. Having learned the components of grammar, the part of communicative competence, the development of languages, and the contribution of Malapropism and Code-Switching, the researcher ensures that learners can now develop/produce a good composition for him/her to face the challenges of being a good writer and speaker. Therefore, it is a great concern of English lecturer to remind the learners of the importance of bilingualism and multilingualism and be more competent in delivering what he/she wants to convey. Malapropism and Code-switching may be an error for both the teacher and the learner. Still, it aims us, English persons, to master English and other languages for academic and professional purposes.*

1. INTRODUCTION

The study of English and foreign languages is a big challenge for both the teacher and the learners. You need to study various theories and methods of language to equip you with the knowledge that is useful to develop learners' skills in reading, writing, listening, and speaking. To be recognized as a competent communicative speaker, one should study bilingualism or multilingualism.

The field of second and foreign language teaching and learning has been an issue of debate for a long time. Various theories and methods of language learning have been introduced. The grammar-translation process occupied the field of foreign and second language teaching for many decades and is still of use today. This field has also been dominated by behaviorist theory and the idea that language is nothing but a social behavior that can be learned like any other behavior through habit formation. Many language drills have been designed for this purpose. Learners may share the same aim of learning a language: 'being able to use it effectively; but which ability is required for that? how to achieve it? have been questions for both linguists and methodologists. (https://cutt.ly/TnzeE4W)

In a Linguisticator blog, Sypros Armostis stated: "If language learner is asked what they think the goal of a language course is, they would probably answer that it is to teach the grammar and vocabulary of that language. However, if they are asked what their goal as language learners is, they would most probably answer that it is to be able to communicate in that language."

Malapropism and code-switching have been very useful techniques in our educational system today. Malapropism may be an error, but once you've translated it, you can derive the words for the learners to clearly understand the actual meaning. Learners being non–native speakers may find it hard to translate some of the English words in Filipino like *"take a bath" "kumuha ng paliguan,"* sing softly"- *umawit ng malambot"*.

The capability of the learners to express themselves today is proof that Linguistic Purpose and Historical Implications of Malapropism and Code-Switching helped educators understand the language of the millennia's terminologies. Filipino millennials have many slang words that the older generation may not easily comprehend but once translated, they can find it easy to understand. *Pinoy* Millennial Slang word *"lodi"* is the perfect *tagalog* slang word for that person you idolize, as reading *lodi* backwards will give you "idol." *Petmalu* is a tagalog slang word that means extreme, exceptional, cool, excellent, or extraordinary. When jumbled up, the tagalog word malupit, also spelled *malupet* will give you the slang word *petmalu. Charot* is another popular word. So popular that there was a list of the most Tagalog slang words, this one would be at the top. Use this hip word when you are joking around; it means "I'm just kidding." (https://cutt.ly/2nztyPT)

Knowing all these languages enables us to cope up with the language of the new generations. Malapropism and code-switching may be interpreted as inappropriate. Still, it can awaken the students' learning capability to easily identify the error in pronouncing a certain word that needs to be corrected.

2. DISCUSSION

In handling English subjects, teachers often have difficulties; reading, writing, and speaking skills. Students are not proficient in the English language, particularly in speaking language. Therefore, English teachers are forced to switch to make the students understand the subject matter. Switching from one language to another language is an effective way to establish classroom communication continuously. Fortunately, the focus of second language teaching has moved from purely teaching grammar and vocabulary to providing effective communication skills. A language course should have linguistic competence as its goal and communicative competence (Spyros, 2013).

Communicative competence is a term coined by Dell Hymes (1966) in reaction to Noam Chomsky's (1965) notion of "linguistic competence". Communicative competence is the intuitive, functional knowledge and control of the principles of language usage. As Hymes observes: "… a normal child acquires knowledge of sentences not only as grammatical, but also appropriate. He/she acquires competence as to when to speak, when not, and what to talk about with whom, when, where, in what manner. In short, a child becomes able to accomplish a repertoire of speech act, to take part in special events, and to evaluate their accomplishment by others" (Hymes 1972, 277).

Language users need to use the language correctly (based on linguistic competence) and appropriately (based on communicative competence). This study (Linguistic Purpose and Historical Implications of Malapropism and Code-Switching in the Philippines) is a great help for us to learn more approaches for the benefit of our learners.

In other words, the language used needs to use the language code, i.e., its grammar and vocabulary, and the conventions of its written representation (script and orthography). The grammar component includes the knowledge of the sounds and their pronunciation (i.e., phonetics), the rules that govern the sound interaction and patterns(i.e., phonology), the formation of words using inflection and derivation (i.e., morphology), the rules that govern the combination of words and phrase to structure sentences(i.e., syntax), and the way that meaning is conveyed through language(i.e., semantics)

Sociological competence is the knowledge of sociocultural rules of use and knowing how to respond to language appropriately. The appropriateness depends on the communication setting, the topic, and the relationships among the people communicating. Moreover, being appropriate depends on knowing other cultures' taboos, what politeness indices are used in each case, what politically correct term would be for something, how a specific attitude (authority, friendliness, courtesy, irony, etc.) is expressed.

Discourse competence is producing and comprehending oral and written texts in speaking, writing, listening, and reading. It knows how to combine language structures into a cohesive and coherent oral or written text of different types. Thus, discourse competence involves organizing words, phrases, and sentences to create conversations, speeches, poetry, email messages, newspaper articles, etc.

Strategic competence is the ability to recognize and repair communication breakdowns before, during, or after they occur. For instance, the speaker may not know a certain word, thus planning to paraphrase or ask what the word is in the target language. During the conversation, background noise or other factors may hinder communication: therefore, the speaker must know how to keep the communication channel open. If the communication was unsuccessful due to external factors (interruptions) or the message is understood, the speaker must know how to restore communication. These strategies may be requests for repetition, clarification, slower speech, or the usage of gestures, taking turns in communication.

These four components of communicative competence should be respected in teaching a foreign language – and they usually are by modern teaching methods employed in second language teaching. Usually, most of the above are best learned if the language learner immerses in a country's culture that speaks the target language (Spyros, 2013).

The author of this study allows us to better understand and reach communicative competence to a great degree, even if the speaker has never been immersed in a target culture. To be communicatively competent, the researcher, an English lecturer, needs to know the components of communicative competence, linguistic competence, which includes the knowledge of the sounds and their pronunciation because what comes to our lips will be adapted by our learners. Therefore, it is the responsibility of the English lecturer to remind learners that in being communicative competent, you don't only need to study bilingualism, but multilingualism as well.

Malapropism and code-switching are very helpful and useful not only for the learners but also for some teachers. We cannot deny that during our discussion/ lectures in English class, we consciously or unconsciously uttered words different from what it used to be. It enables us to recognize bad English and switch to a good/better one.

Malapropism and Code-switching helped us identify the language, making the bad seem good, the negative seem positive, the unpleasant appear attractive.

3. CONCLUSION

The colonization of Americans influenced Filipinos to be very effective in communication, especially since the medium of instruction is English (Estremera, 2021). This contribution of foreign languages enables our mentors to teach the importance of communication that the researcher also wants to share her knowledge with her learners what she has gained from the author. Malapropism and Code-Switching may be encountered in our text or speech. It is expected since we are not proficient enough in foreign languages. What is important is we were able to bridge the gap among learners between the barriers of languages.

Having learned the components of grammar, the component of communicative competence, the development of languages, and the contribution of Malapropism and Code- Switching, the researcher ensures that learners can now develop/produce a good composition to for him/her to face the challenges of being a good writer and speaker. Therefore, it is a great concern of English lecturer to remind the learners of the importance of bilingualism and multilingualism and be more competent in delivering what he/she wants to convey. Malapropism and Code- Switching may be an error for both the teacher and the learner. Still, it aims us, English persons, to master English and other languages for academic and professional purposes.

REFERENCES

Chomsky, Noam (1965). Aspects of the theory of syntax, Cambridge: M.I.T.Press.
Estremera, M. L. (2021, May 19). Linguistics Purpose and Historical Implications of Malapropism and Code-switching in the Philippines. Indonesian Journal of EFL and Linguistics, 6 (1), 169-186. Retrieved May 30, 2021, from

https://indonesianefljournal.org/index.php/ijefll/article/view/35
3

Hymes, Dell H. (1966). "Two types of linguistic relativity" in Bright, W. Sociolinguistics, Hague: Mouton.pp.114-158.

Hymes, Dell H. (1972) "On communicative competence" In Pride, J. B. Holmes, J. Sociolinguistics: selected readings. Harmondsworth: Pequin.pp.269-293.

Lutz, William (2007). "Doubts about Doublespeak" in Exploring Language by Gary Goshgarian. New York: Pearson Longman.

Spyros, Armostis (2013). Communicative Competence Sabri Thabit Ahmed Communicative Competence in English as a Foreign Language: It's Meaning and the Pedagogical Considerations for its Development

9

Linguistic Purpose and Historical Implications of Malapropism and Code-Switching: An Effective Strategy for Language Learning

Synopsis: The Philippines is recognized globally as one of the largest English-speaking nations, with the majority of its population having at least some degree of fluency in the language. English has always been one of the official languages of the Philippines and is spoken by more than 14 million Filipinos. As considered one of the nation's major languages, learning English has been included in the education curriculum even before. Aside from Filipino, English subject is a major discipline that a primary to tertiary level needs to study. Every country wishes to have a competitive citizen, well-versed in or even knows how to use a second language, such as English. In the present situation of the educative process in the Philippines, there is a need to innovate some strategies on how to develop learners who are confident in communicating in English. Educators as facilitators of learning need to create and innovate some ways to aid the existing problem in the English proficiency of the learner in the country. One of these is incorporating Code-Switching and Malapropism in educating the learners, particularly in English subjects. Facilitating this kind of strategy in class will help the students understand the lesson well and develop the learners' communicative skills in the second language. Improving oneself in the English language is an effective weapon in building the path to his/her career.

1. INTRODUCTION

Communication is an important thing that individual needs to develop to be able to be competitive in his/her career. Communication plays a fundamental role in our daily lives. Good communication comes naturally, but it can be harder for others to articulate their thoughts and feelings when conversing, often leading to conflict and fundamental errors. Learning the second language, English, for us Filipinos is quite easy because of the influence of American colonization in the regions of the Philippines.

The Philippines is recognized globally as one of the largest English-speaking nations. The majority of its population has at least some degree of fluency in the language. English has always been one of the official languages of the Philippines and is spoken by more than 14 million Filipinos. As considered one of the nation's major languages, learning English has been included in the education curriculum even before. Aside from Filipino, English subject is a major discipline that a primary to tertiary level needs to study. But despite this, there are still many students who find it hard to engage themselves in the English subject.

2. DISCUSSION

The Philippines fell from 14th place in 2018 and 20th to the 2019 English Proficiency Index (EPI) (Valderama, 2019) and caused a worry that the country's education sector immediately needs to address. EPI measures the average level of English language skills based on the results of an online Standard English Test (SET) administered by English Proficiency Education First, a Swiss-based global company focusing on language, academic, cultural exchange, and educational travel programs. The Department of Education (DepEd), the Commission on Higher Education (CHEd), state universities and colleges (SUCs), and other stakeholders should step up efforts to improve the teaching and learning of English and develop it as a vital skill of the workforce. (Valderama, 2019)

In the present scenario, in many schools in the Philippines, some students taking communication and English subjects find it hard to absorb the subject. In some instances, teachers could not express themselves clearly in English. If the teachers have difficulty articulating, how then the students would be able to learn the subject and learn the language. According to Borabo (2012), Andrew Churches listed eight competencies that a teacher should possess; being the communicator is one. The teacher is described to be fluent in tools and technologies for communication and collaboration.

In today's global world, the importance of English cannot be denied and ignored since English is the most common language spoken everywhere. With the help of developing technology, English has played a major role in many sectors, including medicine, engineering, and education, which is believed to be the most important arena where English is needed (Kasim,2008). Yet, many researchers have proven that the English language proficiency of Filipinos has deteriorated over the years. And this is very evident in the Junior and Senior high school levels. It must be emphasized that English is a skill for communication and not just a set of facts to be learned. With the challenges that the present Education system in the Philippines is facing, teachers need to innovate how they will help the students easily embrace the subject and eventually use the language in communication. Some strategies that the facilitators of learning use are Code-switching and malapropism, which greatly help the learners.

Code-switching, as defined, is a linguistic phenomenon that occurs in multilingual speech communities. The term describes how a communicatively competent multilingual speaker alternates or switches between two languages or language varieties or codes during the same conversation. McArthur (2005) states that code-switching is simply translating a word or a sentence to the native tongue of the learners to understand the thought better that the teacher wants to convey to his/her students. Although inappropriate, code-switching has shown a big impact when it comes to the learners' understanding. They can easily grasp or understand the lesson if it is translated into their language. For instance, a story is well delivered by the reader but does not assure that it was understood by the listeners, especially those students who are low when it comes to comprehension. To facilitate the learning, the teacher will explain the story in the easiest way he/she can and use code-switching. It is an important teaching skill that is the ability to transfer knowledge to learners clearly and efficiently. So code-switching can be a useful tool in the classroom for both teachers and learners (Bista 2010:1).

Another strategy is Malapropism; it is the mistaken use of an incorrect word in place of a word with a similar sound, resulting in a nonsensical, sometimes humorous utterance. (https://en.wikipedia.org). Even if it aims to throw humor to the listeners, it also helps the students recognize words through sounds. Playing with words in the lower years of education is very effective because it can establish retention in the learners' minds. These two strategies, Malapropism and Code-switching, may be inappropriate for the principles of communication but are very helpful in the delivery of education.

3. CONCLUSION

Building a better future is everyone's dream and goal in life. A good communication skill is a big help on how a person will shape his future career. This will it can be made possible by educating her/himself in using the language. A person must not make it in a hurry; it must be step by step. Helping the learners love the second language is a major concern of every educator, as is it said that teachers can make and unmake a child. An educator must know how to innovate ways to deliver the lesson even if it draws a little misinterpretation. In teaching the learners to love the English language, Malapropism and Code-switching is a big help; although it was defined as inappropriate, still it can create an easy and assessable way to learn. The inappropriateness of these strategies will be replaced if the teachers or an educator knows how to cope with this little misinterpretation and will lead to a good and effective way of delivering the process of education. Everyone dreams of a prosperous living, but how will it be possible? A person must learn how to become a competitive person through improving and educating oneself. Language learning may be complicated, but loving language can bring you to a world you could never even imagine.

Reference

Estremera, M. L. (2021, May 19). Linguistics Purpose and Historical Implications of Malapropism and Code-switching in the Philippines. Indonesian Journal of EFL and Linguistics, 6 (1), 169-186. Retrieved May 30, 2021, from https://indonesianefljournal.org/index.php/ijefll/article/view/35 3.

Link Sources

https://www.manilatimes.net/2019/11/18/opinion/columnists/topanalysi s/pinoys-english-proficiency-declines-sharply/656784

https://writepass.com/journal/2016/12/code-switching-the-effects-for-students-and-teachers/#:~:text=An%20important%20teaching%20sk ill%20is,more%20force%20to%20a%20phrase.
http://www.ello.uos.de/field.php/Sociolinguistics/Codeswitching
https://projects.ng/project/malapropism-in-the-use-of-english-language-and-its-effect-on-teaching-learning-of-english-language-among-secondary-school-students-a-case-study-of- English.https://zoek.uk/job-seeker-blogs/the-importance-of-communication-skills-for-career-development

10
Classroom Techniques and Public Policy Proposals Resolving Malapropism and Code-switching in the Philippines

Synopsis: There have been two linguistic phenome and: malapropism Hughes, et al. (2006) differentiate additive and subtractive language processes such that the latter indicates a loss of fluency and vocabulary in the first language when acquiring fluency and vocabulary in a second language, whereas additive language processes nurtures fluency and vocabulary in both languages simultaneously. There are languages with perceived lesser academic and economic value, commonly the languages of colonized societies. This ties in with Estremera (2021)'s findings that colonization is a historical basis for the existence of malapropisms and code-switching in the Philippines. These "lesser" languages are treated in the classroom with the goal of practically replacing skills in it with proficiency in a second, more preferable language. In the Philippines, this "more preferable" language is English. This is proven by the preferential use of the English language as a mode of instruction in basic and higher education, except of course for Filipino materials. Malapropisms and code-switching in the Philippines arise as a result of, respectively: a limited cognitive and semantic understanding of the mistaken words and phrases, and a scarce vocabulary in either of the languages being substituted. A contributing social factor to these linguistic reasons is poverty resulting in limited educational attainment in the Philippines. A two-pronged approach is proposed to resolve the two linguistic phenomena: in the classroom and society. Teaching techniques catering to visual learning may aid in the construction of a mental picture and in identifying the correct spelling of words.

1. INTRODUCTION

Two linguistic phenomena observed in the Philippines are malapropism and code-switching (Estremera, 2021). Malapropism is the unintended substitution of an incorrect word for a similar word resulting in nonsense or comical speech, e.g., the use of "inferior" where "interior" should have been used in "What do I look like, an inferior decorator?" (Jones, 2021). This is most commonly observed in spoken language. Code-switching, then, is the interchange between two or more languages of bi- or multilingual speakers in a single conversation. In a linguistic aspect, these arise as a result of lacking cognitive and semantic understanding of certain words and phrases and a scarce vocabulary (Gardner, 2017).

Given the spoken contexts in which malapropism arises, its presence in the Philippines may be discussed as lacking reading and writing skills. Butuyan (2020) cited a Cagayan education summit which reported that approximately fifteen percent (15%) of basic education students were classified as "non-readers." Social discourses in code-switching involve the perceived educational and economic value of substituting certain languages over others, i.e., Hispanic, Vietnamese, and Filipino are viewed negatively. In contrast, Latin, French and Italian are considered positively (Hughes et al., 2006). Sicam & Lucas (2016) reported that adolescent Filipino bilingual learners prefer the English language over the Filipino language due to the perceived higher stature of English.

Given this, it may be inferred that substituting English words in a primarily Filipino conversation may be more positively appreciated than replacing Filipino words in a mainly English conversation. This paper proposes visual techniques in the classroom and public policies to correct and alleviate malapropism and code-switching in the Philippines. The proposals are based on analyses of historical and social contexts in which the two linguistic phenomena arise.

2. DISCUSSION

2.1 Linguistic Origins of Malapropism

The cognitive aspect in the existence of malapropisms lies in the process of text production. Tincheva (2014) concluded that the main cause of malapropisms stems from the speaker's struggle in mentally picturing or having a definitive construct of the mistaken words. Taking into the context that the highest number of functionally literate Filipinos' mass media exposure to English and Filipino is from watching television (PSA, 2019), it can be inferred that Filipino groups characterized by a limited formal educational attainment may pick up common words and phrases and their contextual usage without necessarily learning their proper definitions. This situation, coupled with Tincheva (2014)'s conclusion, sets up a conducive environment in the Philippines for the occurrence of malapropisms.

2.2 Filipino-English Bilingualism as a Subtractive Language Process

Hughes et al. (2006) differentiate additive and subtractive language processes. The latter indicates a loss of fluency and vocabulary in the first language when acquiring fluency and vocabulary in a second language. In contrast, additive language processes nurture fluency and vocabulary in both languages simultaneously. There are languages with perceived lesser academic and economic value, commonly the languages of colonized societies. This ties in with Estremera (2021)'s findings that colonization is a historical basis for the existence of malapropisms and code-switching in the Philippines. These "lesser" languages are treated in the classroom to practically replace its skills with proficiency in a second, more preferable language. In the Philippines, this "more preferable" language is English. This is proven by the preferential use of the English language as a mode of instruction in basic and higher education, except for Filipino materials. In 2019, Department of Education Secretary Lenor Briones stated that English is even being considered for use as the primary mode of instruction (Olarte, 2019). Cabigon (2015) adds that more than being a more prevalent mode of instruction, English has also become the language of commerce and law in the Philippines

2.3 Visual Classroom Techniques Correcting Malapropism

It is advocated that more strategies catering to visual learning about the semantic use of appropriate words and phrases be adopted to address the reported cognitive and semantic constraints resulting from malapropisms. Given that most Filipinos across rural and urban communities, and ages, are most accustomed to the television as their mass media exposure to English and Filipino (PSA, 2019), it is understandable that the watchers would learn and remember the sounds of the words and the contexts in which they are used. As long as a word sounds similar and has the same number of syllables and metrically, it may be mistakenly substituted for the appropriate word (Estremera, 2021). This lack of semantic understanding may be alleviated by presenting visualizations and the correct spelling of the appropriated words, which are usually substituted in common malapropisms.

2.4 Literacy Programs Alleviating the Basis For The Persistence Of Malapropism

Although the Philippines reports a high level of functional literacy, the general level of educational attainment remains low, with at least 60% of Filipinos not graduating beyond high school (PSA, 2011). Charity Ed (2020) cites poverty as the main reason for the inaccessibility of education, which negatively reflects the literacy rate. Butuyan (2020) also pointed out that only a third of Filipino learners have access to books. These social contexts show how illiteracy and socio-economic challenges serve as the basis for the persistence of malapropism in Philippine society. As a direct response to these problems, it is necessary to enact more literacy and poverty alleviation programs on a societal level, such as book drives, reading programs, public funding on education, job security, and the like.

2.5 Social Perspectives On Code-Switching

Building on Estremera (2021)'s report that the historical basis for malapropism and code-switching in the Philippines is colonization, it follows that the two linguistic phenomena—especially the subtractive language process with which Filipino-English bilingualism is treated in classrooms—contribute to colonial mentality. According to IPL (2020), colonial mentality remains a barrier to Philippine economic development. Therefore, it must be ventured that colonial mentality is challenged by academically and socially treating Filipino-English bilingualism additively and the two languages equally. This may be concretized through social programs requiring the Filipino language in public institutions and the institutionalization of a mother tongue-based mode of instruction. Additionally, code-switching due to scarce vocabulary in either language being substituted may be alleviated by the same literacy program proposed above.

3. CONCLUSION

Malapropisms and code-switching in the Philippines arise as a result of, respectively: a limited cognitive and semantic understanding of the wrong words and phrases and limited vocabulary in either of the languages being substituted. A contributing social factor to these linguistic reasons is poverty resulting in limited educational attainment in the Philippines. A two-pronged approach is proposed to resolve the two linguistic phenomena: in the classroom and society. Teaching techniques catering to visual learning may aid in constructing a mental picture and identifying the correct spelling of words. Literacy improvements and poverty reduction, such as book drives and job security initiatives, are critical to making education more accessible. In addition to these, public policies on the Filipino language may also help build a robust vocabulary in Filipino. An additive language learning approach may also help resolve code-switching due to a limited vocabulary Filipino-English code-switching's negative connotations.

REFERENCES

Butuyan, J. R. (2020, January 27). Crisis of illiteracy (1). INQUIRER.net. Retrieved from https://opinion.inquirer.net/126921/crisis-of-illiteracy-1.

Cabigon, M. (2015). State of English in the Philippines: Should we be concerned? British Council | Philippines. Retrieved from https://www.britishcouncil.ph/teach/state-english-philippines - should- we-be-concerned-2.

Charity Ed. (2020, January 7). How poverty affects education in the Philippines. Next Step Philippines. nextstepph.com/how-poverty-affects-the-education-in-the-philippines.

Estremera, M. L. (2021). Linguistic purpose and historical implications of malapropism and code-switching in the Philippines. Indonesian Journal of EFL and Linguistics, 6(1), 169. https://doi.org/10.21462/ijefl.v6i1.353.

Gardner, A. (2017, November 29). Code switching in the classroom: Convenience or catastrophe? | General e ducator blog. Language Immersion Online | Learn a Language with Videos | FluentU. fluentu.com/blog/educator/code-switching-in-the-classroom.

Hughes, C. E., Shaunessy, E. S., Brice, A. R., Ratliff, M. A., & McHatton, P. A. (2006). Code-switching among bilingual and limited English proficient students: Possible indicators of giftedness. Journal for the Education of the Gifted, 30(1), 7-28. https://doi.org/10.1177/016235320603000102.

IPL. (2020). Colonial mentality in the Philippines. Essays, Research Papers, Term Papers. Retrieved from https://www.ipl.org/essay/Colonial-Mentality-In-The-Philippines-P37T942PJED6

Jones, M. (2021, April 15). 16 of the most famous malapropism examples. Reader's Digest. Retrieved from https://www.rd.com/article/malapropism-examples/.

Olarte, S. E. (2019, December 10). DepEd is considering English as the mode of instruction in primary years. COSMO.PH.

cosmo.ph/news/deped-english-mode-of-instruction- primary-years-a1031-20191210.

PSA. (2011). Education of women and men. psa.gov.ph/content/education-women-and-men PSA. (2020). Functional literacy rate of Filipinos by exposure to different forms of mass media ranges from 92.6 percent to 97.1 percent in 2019. https://psa.gov.ph/content/functional -literacy-rate-filipinos-exposure-different-forms-mass-media-ranges-926-percent.

Sicam, F. P., & Lucas, R. I. (2016). Language attitudes of adolescent Filipino bilingual learners towards English and Filipino. Asian Englishes, 18(2), 109-128. https://doi.org/10.1080/13488678.2016.1179474.

Tincheva, N. (2014). The doctor x-rayed my head and found nothing: The linguistic phenomenon of malapropisms. Language for International Communication: Linking Interdisciplinary Perspectives, 213-225. https://dspace.lu.lv/dspace/bitstream/handle 7/2934/Language-for-international-
2014.pdf?sequence=1&isAllowed=y#page=213

11

Generation Z Perspective: Understanding Malapropism and Code-Switching as their Communicative Strategy

Synopsis: Generation that is marked by the internet. From their time of birth, the internet and cell phones were mostly commonplace. They were born into a fully digital world, connected by the internet. It is part of their homes, their education, and their way of socializing. This generation has perfected using the technologically inflected version of English, considering that they have been brought up during the era of technology (Godwin-Jones 19). This led to unmistakable two versions of English, which enables Gen Z's to have malapropism and code-switching as their communicative strategies. Malapropism occurs coupled with the code-switching linguistic phenomenon. Most of the malapropism episodes that transpired are a prelude to shifting from one language to another. (Estremera 2021). Malapropism and code-switching behaviors are not random, nor is it seen as a sign of linguistic deficiency or inadequacy of Generation Z. Rather, it is a negotiation between language use and the communicative intents of the speakers. Malapropism and Code-switching are employed as a tool to achieve these intents. It is also used to express a range of social and rhetorical meanings. As pointed out by Myers-Scotton (1995), the choices that a speaker makes in using a language are not just choices of content but are 'discourse strategies' (p. 57), that is, the choices are used more to accomplish the speaker's intents than conveying referential meaning.

1. INTRODUCTION

Generation Z, or Gen Z for short, is the generation that comes after Millennials and before Generation Alpha. Researchers and popular media use the mid-to-late 1990s as starting birth years and the early 2010s as ending birth years. Most believe that the oldest of Generation Z are those born in 1995, with the youngest of the generation being those born in 2010. This means that as of 2020, they are between 10-25 years old.

Generation marked by the internet. From their time of birth, the internet and cell phones were mostly commonplace. They were born into a fully digital world, connected by the internet. It is part of their homes, their education, and their way of socializing.

This generation has perfected using the technologically inflected version of English, considering that they have been brought up during the era of technology (Godwin-Jones 19). This led to unmistakable two versions of English, which enables Gen Z's to have malapropism and code-switching as their communicative strategies. Malapropism occurs coupled with the code-switching linguistic phenomenon. Most of the malapropism episodes that transpired are a prelude to shifting from one language to another. (Estremera, 2021)

2. DISCUSSION

Malapropism and code-switching as Gen Z's communication strategy illustrate how they organized, enhanced, and enriched their speech by signaling social relationships and language preference, framing discourse, maintaining context appropriateness, reiterating messages, and showing membership and affiliation with other members of Gen Zs'.

2.1 Signaling social relationships and language preference

Gen Z'ers prioritize their social life, which leads them to have their language preferences. Malapropism and Code-switching indicate power and can also be seen as a tool to demonstrate the social relationships among the members of the said generation. Studies have also shown that speakers tend to use these two communicative strategies to fill in the linguistic gaps in the language of interaction. This indicates that such maintenance arises due to chronic use of the terms, training received in English, the comprehensibility of the words in English compared to the native language, and the availability of the English terms in the speakers' linguistic repertoire.

2.2 Framing Discourse

Another function of malapropism and code-switching of Generation Z is to attract and hold listeners' attention. This is done by framing the discourse using conjunctions like 'so' and 'then,' and routines like 'well,' 'ok' and 'alright.' Members of the said generation tend to have a shorter attention span so in sustaining the attention of the listener they use malapropism and code-switching. According to Koike (1987), this normally occurs at boundaries as an intensifying strategy to emphasize the utterance, hold the listeners' attention and move the action forward.

2.3 Reiterating messages

Malapropism and Code-switching are also used to reiterate messages, repeating what has been said earlier in another language to make the message clearer and understood. Gen Z'ers want to ensure mutual understanding among the listeners. Studies have shown that speakers accommodate and consider other interlocutors' linguistic factors in designing their speech (Giles & Smith, 1979; Bell, 1984; Giles, Coupland & Coupland, 1991). Speakers may diverge and converge their address to accommodate the other interlocutors for effective communication.

2.4 Showing memberships and affiliation

Gen Z'ers also code-switch and use malapropism when they want to establish relationships among them. The speaker's choice of the native vocabulary indicates an effort to develop friendship, affinity, and solidarity with the participants. Due to the widespread use of technology, the members of the said generation wanted to feel that belongingness to be useful as their way of communication.

3. CONCLUSION

Malapropism and -switching behaviors are not random, nor are they seen as a sign of linguistic deficiency or inadequacy of Generation Z. Rather, it is a negotiation between language use and the communicative intents of the speakers. Malapropism and Code-switching are employed as a tool to achieve these intents. It is also used to express a range of social and rhetorical meanings. Myers-Scotton (1995) pointed out that a speaker's choices in using a language are not just choices of content but are 'discourse strategies' (p. 57); that is, the choices are used more to accomplish the speaker's intents than conveying referential meaning.

REFERENCES

Demir, B., & Sönmez, G. (2021). Generation Z students' expectations from English language instruction. Journal of Language and Linguistic Studies, 17(Special Issue 1), 683-701.

Estremera, M. L. (2021). Linguistic purpose and historical implications of malapropism and code-switching in the Philippines. Indonesian Journal of EFL and Linguistics, 6(1), 169. https://doi.org/10.21462/ijefl.v6i1.353

Giles, H., Coupland, N., Coupland, J. (Eds).(1991) Contexts of accommodation: Developments in applied sociolinguistics. Cambridge, MA: Cambridge University Press.

Gumperz, J. J. (1971). Language in Social Groups. Stanford, CA: Stanford University Press

IvyPanda. (2019, November 30). Code-switching and generation z. Retrieved from https://ivypanda.com/essays/code-switching-and-generation-z/

Myers-Scotton, C. (1995). Social motivations for code-switching: Evidence from Africa. Oxford: Oxford University Press.

Oxford Learner's Dictionaries. March 8, 2021. Retrieved March 8, 2021.

Turner, Anthony (2015). "Generation Z: Technology And Social Interest." Journal of Individual Psychology. 71 (2): 103–113. doi:10.1353/jip.2015.0021. S2CID 146564218.

12

Linguistic Purpose and Historical Implications of Malapropism and Code-Switching: An aid to Foreign Students

Synopsis. *To cater to the need to be educated even if it is not their hometown, international students reside in the Philippines for study and education. To easily engage with the education system, Philippine educators incorporate the use of malapropism and code-switching in the delivery of lessons to assure that learning is being given and provided to the Foreign learners. With the help of malapropism and code-switching, learning delivery becomes easier for learners with different languages. Using their native language in the process of education is a big help for them to understand well the lessons not just in higher levels but also in preparatory and elementary foreign learners. Education, therefore, is for all regardless of one's gender, age, status, and nationality—every individual aims to educate him/herself to have a productive way of living. Even if far and separated from their country, foreign students decided to have a little sacrifice just to give themselves a proper education. The Philippines, known as one of the countries in the world with high standards for education, embrace the presence of Foreign learners. For them to be appreciated in the country, the best of education is being provided to all. Even if there is a language barrier, it did not turn into a hindrance to learning and educating themselves. Code-Switching and malapropism became an evident tool on how foreign students learned many things aside from the common lessons inside the classroom and developing themselves in learning the English language.*

1. INTRODUCTION

Science claims that human is the highest form of animals. Only humans can communicate and understand things. Through communication with one another, there is growth and progress. Progress in every aspect of life, like personal, social, and improvement in cultural, economic, and especially, helps us connect to different kinds of people culture and races.

Communication is a complicated thing that individuals need to develop. A good foundation of a country, economy, and society knows how to use and communicate in the Second Language. Hence, a people of a particular country need to engage himself/herself in learning the said language. The Philippines is considered globally one of the largest English-speaking nations and produces several professionals because of the high standard for higher education. The Philippines is a country where many individuals from different nations visit to study. International students such as Koreans, Indians, and other nationalities prefer to study in the county. Professors and teachers in the Philippines make the process easy and enjoyable. Native tongues or their original language are employed as a medium of instruction and English to help foreign students engage in the Philippine educational system. Malapropism and code-switching are helpful in this process.

2. DISCUSSION

MANILA, Philippines— has more than 26,000 foreigners are currently studying in various schools throughout the country, with South Koreans topping the list, according to the Bureau of Immigration. Immigration Commissioner Ricardo David Jr. disclosed that more than 17,000 college enrollees accounted for the bulk of the foreign students while the rest were studying in elementary and high school or taking short-term language courses (Aning,2018). The Philippines is a nice country with a good education system. There are a whole lot of reasons why most foreign students' study in the Philippines; unlike other countries that restrict their medium of instruction to their local language, the Philippines happens to be the direct opposite because both the medium of instruction and the business language is English, thereby making communication a lot easier between foreign students and the citizens. Almost 90% of Filipinos can understand and speak English well, but that does not neglect or relegate their major language, Tagalog.

The Philippines is the 3rd largest English-Speaking Nation in the World, having the Highest English Literacy rate in Asia. For this reason, there are thousands of foreign students enrolled in different universities in the Philippines (hallmarksconsultancy.com). The Philippine Education system offers high-quality education and assures the students globally competitive academic programs, highly skilled professors, and modern facilities that they surely love. Welcoming the use of other languages of other countries such as Korean and Indian is also included in delivering the lessons: to deliver the lesson well to the foreign students, their language is being used in the discussion aside from the English language as a major medium of instruction, and it is considered Code-switching. Foreign students from Korea, Japan, and India find it difficult to communicate in English because of their less exposure to English.

To educate them well, code-switching from English to their language is a must. Code-switching or language alternation occurs when a speaker alternates between two or more languages, or language varieties, in the context of a single conversation or situation. Multilingual speakers of more than one language sometimes use elements of multiple languages when conversing with each other. Thus, code-switching uses more than one linguistic variety in a manner consistent with the syntax and phonology of each variety (https://en.wikipedia.org).

Foreign students are known to be multilingual. Foreign students feel more comfortable when addressed in their native language, making building relationships easier. In the interest of a positive classroom environment may be a good trade-off. They were yet ensuring not to fall into habits by overdoing it. A good point of using code-switching in the classroom with the foreign students is that they learned and got engaged with learning the English language used internationally (en.wikipedia.org). Code-Switching could be used as a stimulus for further developing individuals' home language in the home context.

Aguirre (1988), Hudelson (1983), and Olmedo-Williams (1983) found code-switching to be an effective teaching and communicative technique which could be used among bilingual learners. Malapropism is defined as an amusing error that occurs when a person mistakenly uses a word that sounds like another word but has a very different meaning. Foreign students in the lower years like preparatory and elementary also find it hard to learn the language. To facilitate well learnings in English, Malapropism may be used. The use of fun activities yet interesting is effective to learners. Using words with different meanings but the same sound can also help them build vocabulary by using the hint of a sound to identify a word. Same with code-switching, malapropism should be used minimally in presenting the lesson. For it will deviate from the purpose of the rules of grammar.

3. CONCLUSION

Education is for all regardless of gender, age, status, and nationality—every individual aims to educate him/herself to have a productive way of living. Even if far and separated from their country, foreign students decided to have a little sacrifice just to give themselves a proper education. The Philippines, known as one of the countries in the world with high standards for education, embrace the presence of Foreign learners. For them to be appreciated in the country, the best of education is being provided to all. Even if there is a language barrier, it does not hinder learning and educating themselves.

Code-Switching and malapropism became an evident tool on how foreign students learned many things aside from the common lessons inside the classroom and developing themselves in learning the English language. The philippine education system educates foreign students on what they want to have and helps them improve their communication skills by using the International language. It is not merely teaching them to become professionals but also effective communicators in the English language. Sooner or later, educating oneself will become a bridge to fully realize every country's dream to have a competitive citizen. This will be possible if every individual embraces the love of educating themselves.

References

Aning , Jerome. (2011). Philippine Has 26k Foreign Students, Inquirer Net. (HTTPS://PROJECTS.NG/PROJECT/MALAPROPISM)

Aguirre, A. (1988). Code-switching, intuitive knowledge and the bilingual classroom. In H. S.

Escobedo (Ed.), Early childhood bilingual education: A Hispanic perspective (pp. 31-49). New York: Teacher's College Press.

Estremera, M. L. (2021). Linguistic purpose and historical implications of malapropism and code-switching in the Philippines. Indonesian Journal of EFL and Linguistics, 6(1), 169. https://doi.org/10.21462/ijefl.v6i1.353

García, & R. C. Chávez (Eds.), Ethnolinguistic issues in education (pp. 28-38). Lubbock, Texas: College of Education, Texas Tech University

Hudelson, S. (1983). Beto at the sugar table: Code-switching in a bilingual classroom. In T. H.

Olmedo-Williams, I. (1983). Spanish-English bilingual children aspeer teachers. In L. Elias- Olivares

(Ed.), Spanish in the U.S.setting: Beyond the Southwest (pp. 89-106). Wheaton, Maryland:National Clearinghouse for Bilingual Education.

Link Sources:

Code-switching (https://en.wikipedia.org/wiki/Code-switching)

Why you should consider studying in the Philippines, Hallmark Educational Consultant International (https://www.hallmarksconsultancy.com/)

13

Linguistic Purpose and Historical Implications of Malapropism and Code-Switching in the Philippines: A localized Perspective

Synopsis: This paper examined the when, why, and how codes-witching and malapropism in the Philippines had taken place. "In linguistics, code-switching or language alternation occurs when a speaker alternates between two or more languages, or language varieties, in the context of a single conversation or situation" (en.m.wikipedia.org). "With this definition, code-switching is used by everyone as they change their language style based on who they are talking to, what they are talking about, where they are, and much more. This type of code-switching occurs in social groups, primarily based on age, class, geographic location, upbringing, and ethnicity" (Kenzie Shofner 2021). The following definitions are very much observable in the Philippine context, for Filipinos speak two or more languages and dialects that exist in a particular place. Code-switching can even be traced by the influence of the different cultures, languages, and trends that were considered and inevitably could happen, given that language is dynamic. In the practical classroom setting, English Teachers may have variations on their strategy used whether to accept on not to accept code-switching among their students. "The study of Eldridge (2004) described and analyzed the code-switching of young learners in a Turkish secondary school. It showed that "there is no empirical evidence to support the notion that restricting mother tongue use would necessarily improve learning efficiency, and that the majority of code-switching in the classroom is highly purposeful and related to pedagogical goals. In response, it is reflected that code-switching may have different intentions and effects, thus giving a clear view that it is evident and may not be uncounted. It may provide an answer to questions like why do students or teachers code-switch? How do they code-switch? And when do they code-switch? The following questions can be answered, for they have already been considered in the Philippine setting.

1. INTRODUCTION

"The important thing about speaking another language is it allows you to stand in the shoes of that other culture and see the world from their point of view," states Thomas Zweifel, chief executive of a cross-cultural coaching firm in New York (Coombes, 2004, p. 4). Malapropism and Code- Switching have been very evident in our educational system. It may be viewed as an error, but practically speaking, it served as a stepping stone for our learners to learn English. The ability of a person to create words and finally be acceptable to the norms of a particular setting may be the start of Malapropism and Code-Switching. Understanding and reviewing Malapropism and Code-Switching can hint at understanding our learners instead of depressing the learning process. It can also be some fun or ice breaker in a classroom; for example, you say" maka-iinit ka" instead of saying "You're so hot" in English.

2. DISCUSSION

As secondary public-school teachers handling English, it has always been our target that our learners will develop their reading, writing, and speaking skills at the end of the day. However, the process of doing so comprises lots of challenges and hindrances. First, students being non-native speakers of English may find some words as alien, in a sense that they cannot recognize the appropriate sound or the word itself. Second, students may recognize the word and sound but may not interpret or give meaning to it in terms of comprehension. And based on this paper (Linguistic Purpose and Historical Implications of

Malapropism and Code-Switching in the Philippines), students and Teachers may rely on their last resort of code-switching or malapropism. Career opportunities are lost when you fail to recognize your role in the communication process or use appropriate skills. The ability to talk seems so simple. But, it is not. Once you master the skills of interpersonal and presentational communication, speaking becomes as simple as it looks (Kathryn Sue Young).

The history of how Filipinos found their way/s on understanding the process of learning English as a second language can be very evident in how we are very much conscious of our grammar, pronunciation, and content. In contrast, although some may disagree, the use of code-switching can be of great help to students. Bridging a learner's first language to the presented second language can ease the pain of grasping such. As experienced, students often ask their teachers to translate English sentence/s or word/s into Tagalog or vice versa.

They even unconsciously and mistakenly translate a Tagalog sentence literally to English (kumakain si Pedro sa lamesa – Pedro is eating the table). Sometimes they even interchange the use of an adjective to a verb or a verb to an adjective, for example, "You can summarize the story – You can summary the story." On the other hand, not every child has learned English since childhood, resulting in low recognition and comprehension.

Thus, the responsibility is handed down to teachers. The question is, why do Malapropism and code-switching happen? The study of Thompson (2013) provided reasons why People code-switch.

1. Our lizard brains take over: the most common examples of code-switching were completely inadvertent; folks would slip into a different language or accent without even realizing it or intending to do it. With that, because of peoples' diverse cultures and upbringing, we tend to incorporate our second language with that of our native language for it is really hard to evade what we were used to, right? For example, when our students try to

explain something, they unconsciously say "kasi" to bridge the fact/s with their perspective.

2. We want to fit in: People often code-switch- both consciously and unconsciously- to act or talk more like those around them.
   - For example, you're new in a class, since you wanted to be with your new classmates, you try to examine first how they speak then eventually get into how they also talk.

3. We want to get something: Many people code-switch not just to fit in but to actively ingratiate themselves to others.
   - The main word here is "sympathy," there is, of course, the need to be careful of what one must say, for it can make yourself clear or, unfortunately, not get what you intend.

4. We want to say something in secret: We collected many sweet stories of people code-switching to hide in plain sight, a common habit among people in love.
   - In the Philippine setting, this happens in a very dynamic way. One may use Gay languages or jejemons in speaking or even in writing.

5. It helps us convey a thought: Many people switch languages or employ colloquialisms to express particular ideas. In response, it is a perspective that most people code-switch because it needs to be understood. Sometimes people may not find it satisfying to use their L2; instead, they ultimately rely on their L1. Moreover, people may code-switch depending upon who they are talking with. Since they are familiar with the person, it is a stimulus-response that the speaker can easily convey the thought using their L1.

Furthermore, Salazar (2011), based on an interview, the following reasons for performing code-switching were given by the respondents:

1. Competency related code-switching
   a. The hardship of expressing one's thoughts in L2
   b. Difficulty in translating L1 to L2
   c. Limited L2 lexicon/vocabulary

2. Culturally related code-switching
   a. Everybody does code-switching, and it is normal for everyone

3. Communicative related code-switching
   a. For a better understanding of the listeners and to provide additional inputs and examples
   b. To reiterate an argument and to emphasize a thought/opinion
   c. To adjust to some listeners who might misinterpret the L2 utterance

The above findings validate the result of the Students' Survey by Matila (2009), which provided the following reasons for code-switching:

- Pragmatic self-expression, loss of words (e.g., translation problems, not knowing the right words)
- Speech community influence
- Natural occurrence (habit)
- Exposure to two sets of languages
- Fluency in speaking both languages
- Some words are more pleasing to use in Tagalog than in English and/or the other way around
- To make the person more comfortable in sending messages and for listeners to understand the speaker's text better

3. CONCLUSION

The history of malapropism and code-Switching in the Philippines was already observable long before the Americans arrived. The coping ability of a person to finally survive and learn has something to do with how they learn English as means of communication and transacting to progress. Therefore, it is of great concern as English Teachers to be reminded of the importance of speaking more than one language and being competitive on it. Moreover, may it not be omitted that some of our learners are not being presented with the opportunities to learn English since childhood, where word recognition and comprehension may occur.

Finally, Malapropism and code-switching may exist; however, it is considerable for we are Non-native speakers of English in our context. And, the journey to developing and understanding without code-switching and Malapropism has a clear future, for we had been good in English and ultimately be better at it. "Moreover, educators must not forget that English medium of instruction especially in an L2 classroom should remain to be the language for formal class discussions and code-switching should be regulated to discourage indiscriminate use" (Salazar, 2011).

References

Bautista, Ma. Lourdes S. (2000). An analysis of functions of Tagalog-English code-switching: data from one case. De La Salle University, Manila.

Barlongan, Arian M. (2009). Tagalog-English Code-Switching in English Language Classes: Frequency and Forms. De La Salle University.

Barredo, Inma M. (1997). Pragmatic functions of code-switching among Basque-Spanish Bilinguals. The University of Illinois. Retrieved at: http://webs.uvigo.esl/ssl/actas1997.

Crystal, D. (1987). The Cambridge Encyclopedia of Language. Cambridge University Press: Cambridge. Retrieved at: http://eltj.oxfordjournals.org.

Eldridge, John. (2004). Code-switching in a Turkish secondary school. Retrieved at: http://eltj.oxfordjournals.org.

Estremera, M. L. (2021). Linguistic purpose and historical implications of malapropism and code-switching in the Philippines. Indonesian Journal of EFL and Linguistics, 6(1), 169. https://doi.org/10.21462/ijefl.v6i1.353

Matila, Romylyn A. (2009). Decoding the switch: Looking at classroom code switching as a guide in teaching and learning. Retrieved at: http://www.britishcouncil.org

Salazar, E. (2011). Code-Switching of L2 Learners in English Classroom. Languages and Linguistics. Retrieved from https://bit.ly/39K8lSZ. September 23. 2021.

Schilling-Estes, Natalie. (2007). Sociolinguistic Fieldwork.

Skiba, Richard. (1997). Code switching as a countenance of language interference. Retrieved at: http://iteslj.org.

Thomas, Zweife. (2004). Chief executive of a cross-cultural coaching firm in New York.

Link Sources

Code-switching. https://en.m.wikipedia.org
https://www.unitedlanguagegroup.com Linguistic Code-Switching: What it is and Why it Happens
Five Reasons Why People Code- Switch: Code Switch www.npr.org
Kathryn Sue Young. Oral Communication (Third Edition) www.waveland.com